For Steve and Jen

Amigos!

Reserve America

CID# 6877 67582

# Playing
## in the
# Light

My Journey with the Art of Capoeira

Patrick "Galego" Hilligan

With a foreword by
Mestre Acordeon

Move! Studio Publishing
600 Broadway, Suite D
Sacramento, California 95818
www.adbcapoeira.com


Playing in the Light/ Patrick Hilligan. -- 1st ed.
ISBN 978-0-692-19365-5

Printed in the United States of America

*Dedicated to my parents, who gave me the tools to realize my dreams, and to my teachers, who showed me the way.*

# Contents

# Foreword

I am happy and honored to write the foreword for this book by my capoeira student and friend, Patrick Hilligan. Patrick, known in capoeira as Mestre Galego, has been practicing capoeira with me for twenty-seven years and is one of the few students of his generation to open a school. Over the course of almost three decades, Galego has shown beyond doubt his dedication to the art. His teaching work has contributed significantly to the growth of capoeira in the U.S., especially here in California. Now this book tells his story.

Galego begins this work with his graduation to the level of Mestre de Capoeira, a capoeira ceremony that marked his life forever. Next he travels to the past and reveals his experience as a young man wandering in different parts of the world. When he discovers capoeira and its universe, he establishes a long-lasting bond with the art and his teachers. Absorbed in these pages, I was surprised at the similarity of our feelings and trajectories despite their significantly different cultural contexts.

As Galego's adventures reminded me of my own, my thoughts brought me to the beginning of my journey. Sixty years ago in Bahia, Brazil, on the Caminho do Camugerê, I crossed the steps of the capoeira school of legendary teacher Mestre Bimba (Manuel dos Reis Machado, 1899–1974). I was a white kid growing up in the African-Brazilian culture of Salvador, Bahia—similar in a way to Galego's outsider status. I had no clue what capoeira was beyond a unique blend of fighting techniques and what I saw in popular street festivals. I fell in love with the mystery and depth of this art. It encompasses so many different facets, as a pastime, efficient martial art, and powerful means of self-expression and liberation. Through it, one can dive into the history, rituals, and everyday life of the resilient people who created and sustain capoeira with strength and dignity.

At that time the city of Salvador—called Bahia by its natives—was almost magical, secluded in its beauty and cultural richness. For me, it was the center of the universe. It took time for it to cross the frontiers of my awareness—a captivating and fragile shell, surrounded by enchanted, beautiful beaches, warm weather, and friendly people. I believe that capoeira has allowed me to fly so much farther in my experience of life than I could have without this extraordinary means of association and perception.

One day my mestre, a giant black man who exuded wisdom, told me that capoeira would spread throughout the world like grains of sand on beaches. He noted that "The fruit only ripens at the right time."

Galego's stories and adventures are captivating. His journey to and along the capoeira path displays the ripening of the exotic fruit of Mestre Bimba's riddle. Galego has paid his dues for his time and place and can inspire others to break the constrictions of cultural nearsightedness. What rises above all his many challenges, difficulties, and surprises is the innate pleasure of becoming and being a capoeirista. To be a Mestre de Capoeira is to accept and reinvest in the responsibility to guide and care for the art and one's students. It is to remain a capoeirista in heart and mind. Galego has been faithful in his devotion and confirms his presence as another sand grain among others, on far shores that Mestre Bimba had the clairvoyance to see.

Just as I made a brave leap into the unknown by coming to the U.S. with capoeira, Galego has leapt as well. His commitment to capoeira, made so many years ago, has blossomed into a career. Decades later, he and I are still talking and playing capoeira, intrigued by its never-ending profundity and reach. Enjoy this voyage, in which an unlikely Irish-American guy finds himself at the right place in the right moment to begin his capoeira story and to become a part of capoeira's history beyond Brazil.

Ubirajara Almeida – Mestre Acordeon
December 16, 2017
Berkeley, California

# Prologue

Droning music fills the crowded hall. In the middle of the room, people sit on the floor around a circle of open space. On one side, a row of musicians sings and plays percussion instruments. Everyone wears the same white pants and t-shirt.

Inside the circle, two people whirl and dart. Their movements are explosive and seamless. Cartwheels, handsprings, and spinning kicks stream in rapid succession. After one's foot misses the other's face by inches, the two pull apart for a moment. Swinging side to side, they circle each other like two roosters in a fight.

Suddenly one figure sweeps the legs from under the other, who tumbles toward the floor. Twisting like a cat, she catches herself on her hands, avoiding what might have been a bad fall. There's a gasp from the watching crowd. Then, with an acrobatic spin, she's back on her feet. The two continue their fight-like dance.

Looking around I see familiar faces, including many old friends and some new acquaintances too. This is our *capoeira* community. Capoeira is a traditional art form that includes martial arts, dance, music, and a game of ritual combat. It comes from colonial times in Brazil, born of the African slaves' struggle for survival and freedom. Since then capoeira has come a long way, and it is now practiced around the world. For many, it is a way of life.

It is August of 2013 in Berkeley, California. This event is a *batizado*, a graduation ceremony for capoeira students and teachers. This occasion includes the promotion of three individuals to the level of *mestre*: a master of the art of capoeira. I am one of them. After twenty-three years of training, teaching, playing capoeira, opening my own school, and founding a capoeira group, I am now to be recognized as a mestre.

The music suddenly stops. The two players shake hands and disperse into the crowd. A man stands and speaks. He appears to be in his early sixties, but with a powerful build and straight posture. His hair and thick beard, though, are mostly white. He speaks English with a heavy Brazilian accent, in a low, rumbling voice. Everyone listens intently, but between the accent and background noise, some people struggle to understand his words. Not I, though. I am sitting close, as is my custom, and I have many years of practice trying to understand Mestre Acordeon.

We are in a capoeira academy, a training facility for martial arts, music, and dance. The big, open space is lined with murals, pictures, plants, and musical instruments. This is home to Mestre Acordeon, Mestre Rã, and Mestra Suelly, the founders of the United Capoeira Association—and my teachers. The academy is packed with *capoeiristas* from far and wide, as well as friends and family. There are women, men, and children of all races. Many of the most respected capoeira masters from around the world are here. But among them all, Mestre Acordeon is the most respected and admired. In his career of more than fifty years, he has taught capoeira to generations of students in North America and around the world. He is a prolific published author and musician and wrote the first ever book in English about capoeira. When he holds a big event like this, people come from all over. It is hot, and the air is thick from all the bodies packed in together.

Mestre Acordeon introduces the graduates-to-be, and each speaks briefly. Then the music resumes, and each of them plays the game of capoeira versus one of the mestres. This is part of the ceremony of earning their new ranks and titles. It marks a dozen or more years of training and their graduation from capoeira school. Two of them are my students, the first from my school to achieve this.

The new graduates finish their games, and each receives a new *cordão*, the cord used as a belt and to show rank. As they leave the circle, four women come forward. These are established teachers being promoted to the next rank. This is unusual in capoeira, since only men practiced it until a few generations ago.

After the women speak, play, and receive their new cords, Mestre Acordeon steps to the middle of the circle. I know what is coming next, and I try to calm my nerves. He announces it is time for graduation to mestre level. After a brief talk about what this means, he calls me forward, calling me by my nickname, *Galego*. This word means Galician, a reference to my Celtic roots and light coloring. He also summons Cigano, a teacher from Mexico City, and Jordan, my contemporary from Richmond, California. Together we are far from typical capoeira mestres. Behind us sits a long row of more traditional mestres, nearly all African Brazilian.

When it's my turn, I take the microphone and a deep breath. Sticking to my plan, I thank the many people who have taught me or supported me through the years, especially my teachers and parents. I try to express humbleness and a sense of responsibility in taking this title.

I had wanted to take this opportunity to explain myself, and why I'd made this journey with capoeira, if it was possible to do in just a few lines. "When I was a kid, I never knew what kind of job I wanted to grow up into. But did I know that I wanted to find a career that was three things: fulfilling, unique, and it somehow made the world a better place. When I discovered capoeira, I knew almost right away that it was all of this." There are understanding nods in the audience. "Now I've been in it twenty-three years, and it's been a dream come true."

Finally, I express my gratitude to my students. Without their dedication, my career never could have happened. Many of them are here, and they come forward from the crowd now to join me. They wear matching t-shirts with our logo and my new title, Mestre Galego. One of my first students, Bode, takes the microphone and says some kind words about me. Man, I'm so grateful for these guys.

Jordan and Cigano make their speeches, and now it is time now for the mestre's *roda*, where the three of us will play capoeira with the many mestres there. I'm excited—my first roda as a master among masters. Stepping into the circle, I shake the hand of a Brazilian mestre. We cartwheel into the circle and into a familiar step. Now we are the whirling and darting figures, playing the game of capoeira.

I discovered capoeira when I was eighteen years old. I had never heard of it, but back then, hardly anyone outside Brazil had. There were only a handful of capoeira teachers in all of North America, and this was long before its appearances in popular media like the game Tekken 3 and the film *Only the Strong*. From the moment I first saw the spectacular movements and live music of this unique art form, it captivated my imagination, and I knew that capoeira would be a big part of my life. The next year I moved to Berkeley and started taking classes, embarking on a journey that continues to this day almost three decades later.

# PART ONE

# Seek

# CHAPTER ONE

# Israel

"Dad, it's me, Patrick," I said into the payphone. "Son, are you okay?" My father's voice sounded distant and staticky. He was on the other side of the globe, in California.

"I'm fine, Dad. I'm here in Israel, on a kibbutz."

"You made it safely, then. Everything working out?"

The answer was technically yes, but it didn't feel that way. I was alone and scared, and felt like I was in over my head. For a moment, I couldn't speak.

"Patrick?"

My voice cracked as my last resolve crumbled. "Dad, I don't know if I can do this. I'm alone and afraid."

"Afraid of what? What's going on?"

"It's just that I don't know what I'm doing. I don't know what I'm doing here."

"Ah. You're overwhelmed and homesick?"

"Yes, but it's more than that. Maybe I made a mistake." My courage had broken. This adventure, which I had wanted so badly, did not seem grand anymore. "I think maybe I should come home," I conceded in shame.

It was 1989, and a few months earlier back in California I had turned 18. Upon doing so, I promptly informed my father and my high school dean that I intended to drop out of school to travel abroad. There were just a few months of classes left before graduation, but I was impatient and determined. I couldn't see why I shouldn't immediately pursue my dreams of international travel and adventure.

Needless to say, my dad and the dean were not in favor of my plan. They advised me to wait a few months, finish high school, and then go on my journey. This made sense, but I was young, reckless, and stubborn. I insisted I would no longer attend school. My father managed to keep calm and eventually persuaded me to finish my courses through independent study before embarking on my big trip. So I did —and received my diploma in a few weeks, while preparing to travel.

My plan was to work on a kibbutz in Israel, with possible side ventures to Africa or in the Middle East. A kibbutz is a communal settlement, cooperatively organized around agriculture and industry. Each kibbutz has about 500 to 1,000 residents. It includes simple living quarters, basic infrastructure, a manufacturing plant, usually one large dining hall, and a few recreational facilities. Kibbutzim are usually in rural, agricultural areas. I had heard about them when our family had lived in Italy, and my older sister Erin had visited one. The kibbutz hosts "volunteers" from any friendly country who work in exchange for room and board.

My goal was to travel for at least three months, but I only had $1,600. After buying a plane ticket, I would only have a few hundred dollars left. But a kibbutz would provide food and shelter. From there I could see what else I could afford to do.

Israel was unknown, exotic. From traveling with my family, Europe and the U.S. had become somewhat familiar. Israel was in the Middle East and bordered North Africa—a unique country at the confluence of diverse cultures. It was the land of the Bible and ancient civilizations. From the antiquities through modern times, it had been at the center of many historical events. It was within reach of other interesting places, including Egypt with its pyramids, Nile, and Valley of the Kings. Israel was an ideal destination for me with its fascinating history and culture, free kibbutz living, and most people speaking English.

I called the kibbutzim office in San Francisco and confirmed that they would accept me as a volunteer. They told me to check in at their Tel Aviv office when I arrived. There I could choose from the kibbutzim with openings for volunteers. My passport was ready with an Israeli visa, and I bought a round-trip ticket to Tel Aviv, leaving me with $800 in cash and traveler's checks. I could use the return plane ticket at any time in the next year—my precious lifeline. But the plan was to stay abroad for at least three months. I bought an army surplus canvas backpack to carry a few clothes, toothpaste, a toothbrush, a couple of books, and my treasured leather motorcycle jacket. I never wore that damned jacket because Israel was too hot, but I carried the heavy thing around the whole time.

My day of departure arrived in April. I could hardly believe I was going through with it, but there was no turning back. My friends thought I was either bluffing or crazy and seemed surprised when I was actually on my way. My parents had given up trying to change my mind and did what they could to support me, making sure I had a plan, documents, and essential gear. This was it—I was finally off on the adventure I so craved. This was long before the internet, cell phones, or other modern forms of electronic communication. There would be no instant information resource or way to reach me. I would only be able to contact people through pay phones or physical mail, which would take weeks. I would be truly on my own, with only my wits to rely on. But there was nothing holding me back except fear and conventional wisdom, so I went for it. I boarded my plane at the San Francisco airport.

I arrived in Tel Aviv on a weekday morning. The hazy, smoggy air smelled different from California. Security in customs was tight, and everyone was searched. Soldiers armed with assault rifles stood around. They were ubiquitous in Israel, as almost everyone was required to serve in the armed forces for two years starting at age eighteen, and every soldier was required to carry his or her rifle at all times. Half the soldiers were women, which impressed me. At that time the U.S. military did not allow females in combat positions.

Emerging onto a bustling avenue, I managed to catch a bus to a youth hostel. It was a narrow, five-story building with six or eight bunks per room and one bathroom per floor. A cafe and bar on the roof looked over the Mediterranean Sea. I was happy to discover they served beer to eighteen-year-olds.

I had arrived on a Friday, and the kibbutz office was closed until Tuesday, so I spent the weekend on my own. Three days passed slowly as loneliness set in and my strict budget limited activity. When the office opened, I chose among several kibbutzim, none of which I knew anything about. I decided on Kibbutz Reshafim, located south of the Sea of Galilee near the Jordan River—mostly because of its proximity to these interesting bodies of water. I gathered my things and caught a bus to Beit She'an, the town nearest the kibbutz.

After a couple hours' drive through dry landscapes, the bus arrived at Beit She'an. It was a small town, quiet and painted in muted colors. The Jordanian border was in sight just across the valley floor. In between was a patchwork of farms. I ordered a hummus plate at a small café and asked for directions to the kibbutz. It was a five-kilometer walk from there. I started down the dusty road, passing between fields and irrigation ditches. I was nervous, hoping the kibbutz was expecting me, was where it was supposed to be, and had a place for me to stay.

Eventually I came upon the kibbutz—a collection of low buildings and tree-lined walkways enclosed by a tall, chain-link fence. A sign over the large gate read, "Kibbutz Reshafim." I passed through the gate and walked down a long driveway. At first I saw no one— it seemed like a ghost town. It turned out it was dinnertime, so everyone was in the dining hall.

Finally I found a man who took me to the volunteer coordinator, a kindly, middle-aged woman who spoke perfect English. She showed me to my bunk-room, where I deposited my bag, and then to the large dining hall, which was crowded with people eating and talking. I was led to a table where the other volunteers sat—about a dozen backpackers from Europe and Australia, mostly in their twenties. They were speaking English, but I could barely understand a word they said. Their accents were strong and so different from what I was used to. They good-naturedly introduced themselves and attempted to make conversation with me, but I could not understand them. I said a few things, but they had trouble understanding me as well. It was the same with most of the Israelis. It took several days for me to be able to converse with anyone at all. After an awkward moment, I excused myself to go to the self-serve buffet.

The food included raw onions, tomatoes, and cucumbers along with feta cheese and white bread. That was it— nothing else. The spartan fare surprised me, but I was shocked to discover this was the sole menu for breakfast and dinner every single day. Lunch was the same, but with the addition of some stewed meat, potatoes, and other tubers. The austere diet took some getting used to. Eventually though, I came to enjoy finding different ways of slicing, dicing, and combining the vegetables and cheese each day.

I was in a kind of fog throughout the first night and day, stupefied by sensory overload. I absentmindedly went through an orientation, settled into a shared room with a couple of English travelers, and began work.

On the third day, I suddenly hit a wall of culture shock. I was just a kid—in a foreign country, halfway around the world from everything familiar. I had no friends or family there, everything was strange, and I couldn't communicate with the people around me. If something happened to me, nobody would know for weeks. I was frightened, alone, and homesick. All I kept thinking was, *what the hell am I doing?*

After a few hours of near panic, I walked to the sole payphone booth on the kibbutz out by the front gate. Dialing the operator, I asked to make a collect call to my father in California. After a long pause, I heard my father's voice accepting the call.

After my emotional admission of defeat, my father paused for a long moment. When he spoke, his voice was caring but firm. "Patrick, I know it's hard for you right now, and I'm sorry. But you told everyone that you would do this for at least three months. You wanted this experience. You wanted to see the world. I think you should stick it out and stay there. It will get better."

This was not what I wanted to hear at that moment. At the same time, the part of me that still believed in my vision felt vindicated and strengthened. I knew he was right. I had gone to great lengths to make this trip happen. It was the first step of a greater journey to actualize an extraordinary life. If I cut the trip short now and headed home, I would regret it. It would be to accept defeat, give up on my dreams, and resign myself to a life of normalcy. Normal was fine. Many people seemed content with normalcy, and that was great. But it wasn't for me. I wanted anything but normal.

I had to finish this trip to prove to myself, if no one else, that all my ideas about adventuring and living an extraordinary life were not just talk. I realized then that this was a important moment for me. I had to suck it up, and stick it out.

Calming myself, I steadied my voice. "You're right, Dad. I'm going to stay, at least for three months."

"I think you'll be happy you did."

"Thank you for reminding me of what I have to do."

We said our goodbyes. I still felt isolated, but had regained my resolve. I would be fine. There were bound to be hardships in any adventure, but there would be good times too. I had to hang on and push through. I felt grateful to my father for being strong for me. This was the only contact I would have with anyone I knew until I returned to the U.S. three months later.

Each kibbutz dormitory room housed three to four people. After a week, two Americans replaced my English roommates. Jeff and Sharon were Jewish-American college students on vacation, making the obligatory tour of the motherland. Jeff was a short, funny, amiable guy who quickly took me under his social wing. Sharon was almost as gregarious as Jeff, quick-witted, and pretty. As the three sole Americans there, we bonded quickly.

I worked at the small rubber hose factory they ran on the kibbutz. Six monotonous hours coiling and bundling hose each day, broken only by the midday meal. After work each day, young people from the kibbutz and volunteers went to the recreational facilities, which included a pool and a basketball court. All the Israelis seemed to be tall, athletic, and good-looking. The volunteers were a motley bunch, including us Americans, several backpackers from Australia and New Zealand, two or three from Britain, and a few more from Germany, Norway, and France. Volunteers constantly rotated through, due in part to a three-month limit on their stays.

We organized a water polo game, and I quickly learned how strong and fast the Israelis were. It was the volunteers versus the Israelis, and the Israelis utterly dominated us. Humiliated, the older and more diverse volunteers sought redemption in the sport of basketball. I thought with Americans on our team we might have an edge, but that hope was soon destroyed as the Israelis again ran circles around us and scored at will. We were forced to admit that the Israelis were, in fact, simply more athletic than the rest of us.

After several weeks of living and working on the kibbutz, Jeff, Sharon, and I were ready to blow off some steam, and hungry for familiar culture. We heard about an Eric Clapton concert in a town about an hour away and made plans to go. Taking a public bus to the outdoor auditorium, we walked through the gates as the sun was going down. The stands were packed and the energy was high, with a steady buzz from the crowd. Clapton was in a career peak at that time and had a big following in Israel. We found a spot on the grass to the stage's side. A large band came onstage, including a horn section and a trio of backup vocalists. As they launched into the first song, there was a roar of applause, which grew louder when Clapton appeared. The musicians were masterful, it was rock and roll we knew, and soon we were on our feet dancing. When they sang our favorite song, "Layla," we cheered and twirled madly around each other. The Israelis watched us with cautious amusement.

Somehow Sharon had acquired a tiny bit of hashish before leaving the kibbutz. We smoked it right there on the lawn at the concert. There was so little it would not go far, and Sharon said to conserve the smoke by reusing it. I didn't know what she meant but agreed as she took a large hit.

Then she pulled me to her and planted her lips on mine, kissing me. I was surprised but responded in kind. As she opened her mouth, I opened mine, and she blew the smoke into my lungs. After that I was really high, but from the smoke or the kiss I wasn't sure and didn't care. I knew we were just friends, but I couldn't help but have a crush on Sharon.

Every other Friday, the kibbutz held a party in a converted bomb shelter for the young folk. In the small underground room, Israeli youths mingled with international volunteers, drinking beer and dancing. They played mostly hits from the '70s, and a few from the '80s. When Guns N' Roses came on, we Americans sang wildly along. In Israel at the time, Cat Stevens, Pat Benatar, and The Police were big, as well as Eric Clapton of course. But the song the Israelis loved most at that moment was Bobby McFerrin's "Don't Worry, Be Happy," which sounded good to me.

# CHAPTER TWO

# Early Life

I was born on a U.S. Navy base in 1971 in Great Lakes, Illinois, the third of four children and the only boy. My father, Thomas James Hilligan, was born in 1935 and was an officer and lawyer in the Navy for twenty-five years. My mother, Valerie Anne Hope, was born in 1944. She was from Los Angeles, and it is through her we are related to Bob Hope, my great-great-uncle.

Every few years my dad was re-stationed to a new Navy base, so our family moved frequently. By the time I was six, we had lived in Illinois, Rhode Island, Virginia, and Illinois again. During our second stay in Illinois, we lived in a rural area outside a small town called McHenry. There, before I began second grade, my parents took me and my sisters out of public schools in favor of homeschooling. Our mom gave us lessons, and we had plenty of books and educational games. We also had an abundance of free time. In the summer we climbed trees, fished, and ran around in the nearby woods. In the winter we skated on the frozen lake, sledded down snow-covered hills, and learned to ski on a tiny hill near our house.

Learning to read early, I devoured adventure stories like *The Chronicles of Narnia, A Wrinkle in Time, The Adventures of Huckleberry Finn,* and *Hero and Folk Tales of Ancient Ireland.* I yearned to have adventures of my own and dreamt of traveling to far-off lands. Instead I explored the woods, lakes, pastures, and abandoned barns around our neighborhood with an active imagination.

On a cold January day when I was about seven, a storm dumped several feet of fresh snow, draping everything in a thick white blanket. Flakes fell throughout the day. In the warmth of our home, my family settled into indoor activities in the large living room. My younger sister Valerie used her keen eye for aesthetics to color in a geometrical design in an advanced coloring book. My older sister Mora and I halfheartedly attempted to put together a jigsaw puzzle, making each other laugh with ridiculous faces. Eventually she went to join Erin, our eldest sister, who stood by the old turntable searching for something new among the well-worn record albums. I went to the window and stared at the white landscape.

After getting permission, I bundled up in a mass of winter clothing to play outside. Emerging from the house I felt the freezing air sting my face, but I was warm and comfortable in all the protective layers. I walked down the long driveway. Everything was transformed! Our yard was a perfectly even, fuzzy white sheet. Cars and bushes had become massive soft, white mounds. Trees and houses supported thick mantles. The air was still except for gently falling, big white flakes. Nobody was around, and our road was snowed in, preventing traffic. There was near total silence and an unordinary calm. Nature's power and beauty were in abundant display. It was mysterious and a little scary, and I loved it.

After trudging slowly through the thick powder I lay down on the ground, a fluffy white bed. Staring up at the sky, I watched individual snowflakes as they fell toward my face. It felt like I was floating in a frozen cloud. I was delighted, enveloped in the elements. I felt so tiny and vaguely aware of my own fragility. It felt like a thrilling adventure to explore this frozen, peaceful, terrifying, and beautiful environment.

I continued to the base of a hill where there was a large snowbank from an earlier storm. Along with the neighborhood kids, my sisters and I had built a snow fort out of this bank, complete with walls, tunnels, and snowball reserves for future battles. Now I had the fort to myself. Utilizing the new snowfall, I fortified and added to the walls, constructing new enclosures and barricades.

Eventually I headed back to the house. As I approached, I saw my mother watching me from a window. When I came inside, she helped me remove my many layers of clothes.

"Did you have a good time?" she asked.

"Yes," I responded simply.

"Are you cold?"

"No, I'm warm."

"What were you doing out there?"

"Just playing, looking around." I was so shy and quiet when I was a kid. Rarely did I talk at length.

"You like being outside, don't you?"

"Yes. I like the snow."

"That's good, Patrick. It's so good to be connected to nature. I'm happy you appreciate it. When you grow up, hold on to that connection."

"Uh, okay."

My mom continued, "If nature makes you happy, go with that. Wherever life takes you, go with what makes you happy, especially if it makes the world a better place. Follow your bliss. Do you know what that means, Patrick? To follow your bliss?"

"No."

My mom lowered herself to my level and looked me in the eye. "It means to do what makes you happy and fulfilled. It means if you stay true to yourself, you can make your dreams come true."

This was over my head at that early age, but my mom would repeat the sentiment many times, and I took it to heart.

In 1980 the Navy moved our family to Naples, Italy, giving us a taste of the adventure I craved. We rented a large apartment in a walled estate overlooking the Bay of Naples. The property was ancient and ornate, including several houses and beautifully sculpted gardens. Steep terraces led down to the water, where there were more gardens, caves, and a stone pier. There were paths and stairs crossing and recrossing each other, plus stables, hidden passages, and ruins. Across the Bay, majestic Mount Vesuvius with its distinct crater profile reminded us of past eruptions.

After the excitement of exploring the estate wore off, home life became dreary with little to do. But when our father didn't have to work, our family visited historic and notable sites all over the region. We walked through the ruins of Pompeii and climbed into Mount Vesuvius's crater. In Rome we saw the Vatican's opulent halls and toured the Coliseum, where the gladiators had fought thousands of years before. On the island of Capri, we took a boat inside the sparkling Blue Grotto and saw what had been the summer home of Emperor Tiberius. We climbed castles of the Middle Ages, swam in the clear blue Mediterranean Sea, and skied in the Italian Alps. On short trips utilizing military "space available" flights, we visited London, the Greek isle of Corfu, and Germany. Branching out from Spain, we took a day trip to Morocco, my first time in Africa.

Seeing so much of the world at such a young age made a big impression on me and stoked an already active sense of wanderlust and adventure. It was exciting and fascinating to see the dramatic range of scenery and cultures. But it also made me feel inconsequential, anonymous, and small, in the great mass of humanity. I felt a vague angst thinking that someday, when I was dead and gone, my life might be essentially indistinguishable from many others and thus quite forgettable. I thought, *Is there anything special about me at all?* Is there anything inherently special about any of us? I wasn't sure, but I hoped there was. I knew I wanted to do something noteworthy, something remarkable and unique.

My parents had been married twenty years but had long since fallen out of love. When my father retired after a twenty-five-year career in the Navy, they divorced. The family split up and bounced around Europe for a few more months before we all returned to the U.S., me with our father, my sisters with our mother.

My father and I went back to our old house in Illinois while he worked on selling it. It was 1983 and I was almost twelve. We spent the frigid winter preparing for my reintroduction to public school. My dad tutored me when he wasn't busy looking for a job. He occasionally left me alone for a couple of days as he traveled to different parts of the country for interviews. Already independent, I cooked, cleaned, and otherwise looked after myself.

The house sold in the spring, and we headed west to rendezvous with my mom and sisters. They were in Las Vegas, where my mother was pursuing her postgraduate degree. My father and I made the cross-country road trip in his old Volkswagen camper van. It was stuffed full of furniture and luggage and moved slowly down the highway. We took the southern route through Missouri and Oklahoma, chugging through endless prairies.

Driving through the Texas Panhandle on Interstate 40, the landscape seemed to go on forever, perfectly flat plains extending in all directions. The blue sky was huge. Our car seemed minuscule amid this immense expanse. I felt we were exposed and vulnerable, as if the absence of any protruding feature in the landscape would somehow allow the open sky to suck us up.

Scanning the horizon for anything to break the monotony, I saw what seemed to be haze or smoke ahead. It grew quickly, becoming a great wall of dust bearing down on us. My father directed me to close all the windows—this windstorm was about to hit. There was nowhere to escape, no sheltering building, hill, or depression.

The storm front took over the sky and swallowed everything before us. A powerful wind slammed our little van, tilting it at a precipitous angle. Swirling dust obscured our vision and seeped through the cracks around the doors and windows. Still we continued, struggling to get through the maelstrom. Gales screamed and broke upon us, and we could no longer see the highway. Finally we had to pull over. Waiting nervously, I hoped the wind would not tip the van onto its side. My father assured me we would be okay, but his face showed worry. After several hours of pounding wind and inescapable dust, the storm abated, and we gratefully resumed our journey.

Eventually we entered New Mexico's hilly country, happy to be off the Great Plains. After passing through Albuquerque, we stopped in the town of Gallup, exhausted after a long day of driving. Gallup was a ragtag collection of businesses and residences scattered along Highway 40, seemingly little more than a way-stop for truckers and travelers. We checked into a roadside motel and went to sleep.

Early the next morning we loaded up the van as pink fingers of light reached across the sky. The parking lot was full of cars, but we were the only people. Then a man appeared, walked toward us, and stopped a few yards away. He appeared to be in his twenties. He had a light blond beard and carried a small suitcase.

Suddenly he reached into his jacket, pulled out a pistol, and pointed it at us. As we stood there stunned, he demanded, "In the car now!" He looked at my father. "You drive. The boy's with me in the back."

My father realized that if we followed the man's orders, he could take us anywhere and do what he liked with us. Away from town and other people, we would be even more vulnerable. He stood his ground, refusing to enter the van as the man repeated his demands. At a moment when the would-be carjacker glanced away, my father threw the van keys onto the motel roof.

When the man realized what had happened, he went into a rage, cursing us and waving the gun wildly. I was frozen in fear. My father talked to the man, trying to convince him to move on. The gunman would hear none of it. Threatening to shoot us, he told my dad to go and look for the keys.

The motel was one-story in the nearest section and two-story in an adjoining wing. Dad could access the single-story roof by going up the stairs. He reluctantly walked up the stairs, climbed over the railing, and went onto the roof. He was momentarily out of sight when he found the keys. He hid them and returned empty-handed.

When he returned, he said he couldn't find the keys. With increasing anger and frustration, the gunman ordered me to go look for them. I went onto the roof but could not find them, as they were no longer there. I was confused and frightened and wondered if there was a way to escape. But my dad was still with the robber, so I headed back downstairs. When I returned without the keys, the tension increased.

The man did not believe that my father didn't know where the keys were. He accused Dad of playing games and threatened to shoot him. At this point they were standing face to face, while I stood a few yards behind the stranger.

Suddenly my dad said, "Run, Patrick. Run!"

I stayed where I was. I had no idea what to do, but I wasn't going to leave my dad. The carjacker turned to face me.

My father exclaimed in frustration, "Damn it boy, when I say run, you run!"

The gunman realized then that one thing would leverage my father's cooperation. He grabbed my arm, pulled me to his chest, locked his arm around my neck, and set his revolver against my temple. For a moment I could see the bullets in the cylinders. Later I learned it was a .38 Special.

My father pleaded for my release. The bandit tightened his grip and seemed ready to blow my head off. Suddenly a voice called out from behind the carjacker. It was the hotel manager, asking if everything was all right. He had no idea what was going on but had heard talking and climbing on the roof.

In surprise, the would-be-carjacker released me and spun around to face the manager. Immediately my dad grabbed me and roared, "Run!"

As we dove between parked cars, a gunshot blasted behind us, the bullet singing over our heads. We ran wildly through the lot, zigzagging among cars. Another shot fired, and the bullet ricocheted off something nearby. We ducked farther down and kept running. Four more shots rang out from behind us, each missing us as we dove and sprinted toward the highway.

Soon we were around the building's corner and on the highway. We kept running without looking back, lungs burning, fueled by adrenaline and fear. When I slowed, my dad grabbed me by the arm and dragged me along. Nobody was around, so we rushed into a neighboring hotel to look for help or a phone to call the police.

Bursting into the front office, my dad told the office clerk what was happening. As the young man listened, an excited and strangely happy look came over his face. He asked us exactly where this had happened, then pulled a handgun from under the desk and ran out toward the scene of the crime. We watched him go in amazement and stupefaction. I guess he intended to take care of the situation himself. My father picked up the office phone and called 911. We hunkered down behind the desk and waited for the police, afraid to show our faces on the chance the bandit was coming after us.

Eventually the police arrived and secured the area. We retrieved the keys from where Dad had hidden them. Our VW was untouched. The attacker had fled and was still at large. Luckily the hotel manager was fine, and we were unharmed. After giving the police all the information we could, we were dismissed to continue on our journey. The police caught the guy later that day. It turned out he was already wanted for bank robbery and attempted murder.

When we finally resumed our drive it was still only midmorning. My father and I were amazed to be no worse off after the encounter. I held my breath as we drove, afraid to believe we had escaped. I kept looking at our van's shadow on the ground to see if the guy was clinging onto the roof or underneath the car. We were eager to get out of Gallup and New Mexico by this point and drove about as fast as the old VW would go. Only after we crossed into Arizona did I begin to relax.

After we met up with my mother and sisters in Las Vegas, my older sisters Erin and Mora moved with our mom to San Francisco, while my younger sister Valerie and I moved with our father to Nevada City, California. He had been hired there as an assistant district attorney of Nevada County.

Nevada City is a small town in the rural Sierra Nevada foothills, gold country. My sister and I went to the local middle school, where she started seventh grade and I eighth, and we both began a painful introduction to American preteen society. I had spent the ages of six through eleven mostly on my own, without the company of children my age. I had read books, wandered the woods of Illinois, and explored ancient Mediterranean ruins. I had no idea how to fit in with kids at an American public school.

My clothes fit badly. They might even have been hand-me-downs from my sisters. The language of California '80s youth like "rad" and "gnarly" meant nothing to me. I had no friends at first and wasn't even on the social ladder. I felt overwhelmed and intimidated.

This was my first experience of formal education in five years, and my academic performance was mixed. I did well in reading, history, and geography, but I was terribly behind in math and writing. I caught up after a few years and eventually became a B student in high school.

In high school I eventually gathered a few friends. We were far removed from the popular circles at school, all misfits and oddballs—geeks, rebels, and independent thinkers. Ian and Lenny were two kindly guys who remain friends to this day. Damon was passionate about environmental and social justice, always fighting the good fight. His girlfriend Lana was probably the only Asian American at our school. John was Damon's rebellious punk rock brother, wild and angry. I liked his refusal to conform to expectations. Val was the intellectual among us, always exploring new music, literature, and art. And then there was the geeky kid who talked with an odd accent: me. People sometimes asked where my accent was from, but I didn't know. Perhaps it was a mix of many.

We went to see whatever bands might visit our small town. I had a leather motorcycle jacket and bad haircut and jumped in the mosh pits at punk shows. Slamming my body against the other kids at an Agent Orange show I lost a front tooth, banged out on someone's skull. Occasionally we piled into somebody's car and made a road trip to Sacramento or the Bay Area to see bands like U2, David Bowie, and Metallica. When Jane's Addiction played at a small venue in San Jose, we all wanted to go, but there wasn't enough room in the car. So I made the trip curled up in the trunk. At some show at the Crest Theatre in Sacramento, the opening act was a group nobody had heard of yet called Nirvana.

There was talk about what we were going to do with our lives and careers. I had no idea, but I knew one thing: none of the jobs I saw or heard about appealed to me. I felt more than ever that I had to do something extraordinary, as in, literally, not ordinary. I wanted to explore new territory, to do something unique. It was never fame or fortune I desired, I just wanted to do something remarkable, something different than everyone else. This was my life, the one and only, and I wanted it to be exciting, impactful, and unlike any other. And for me, whatever I did to make it all this had to be about substance, not just style, doing, more than talking, and a way of life, rather than a hobby. That meant, to me, that it had to include my day job. That was a problem, because most professions, by definition, include many practitioners. I wanted to find something that had never been done.

I was aware of politics and world events as a teen, or at least beginning to be. My friends and I talked a lot about social and environmental exploitation. Apartheid in South Africa was a big issue of the day. We dutifully boycotted companies that did business there, and Nelson Mandela was our hero. We believed in preserving the natural environment, and books like *The Monkey Wrench Gang* by Edward Abbey and *Ecotopia* by Ernest Callenbach stoked our outrage at its destruction. For me it was authors Steinbeck and Chekhov who clued me into how the rich thrive at the expense of the poor. I had to find a livelihood that didn't support any of this.

My job had to be about making the world a better place, not just about getting a paycheck. And in addition to making a positive impact, and being unique, I wanted my work to be enjoyable in and of itself. If at all possible, I wanted my job to involve some form of play. At this time I didn't even know capoeira existed, much less that it would give me all of this.

In the meantime, I craved experience, knowledge, and adventure. I wanted to explore the world, take risks, and discover the unknown. My travel bug was stoked by books like Lonely Planet's *Africa on a Shoestring*, Carl Franz's *The People's Guide to Mexico*, and Jack Kerouac's *On the Road*. I was in a hurry because I was impatient, and because I feared being lulled into complacency. So I began planning adventures of my own.

# Egypt

Sharon and Jeff soon left the kibbutz for their return to the U.S. We vowed to stay in touch, a promise none of us kept. My new roommates were two amiable Irishmen. Albert, from County Cork in the Republic of Ireland, was stout with dark hair and eyes, a rich baritone voice, and a playful sense of humor. Eugene, from Belfast in Northern Ireland, was slighter and quieter, with dirty blond hair and a reserved demeanor. They had met while living in London and decided to visit the Middle East together. The three of us easily became good friends. We decided to travel together for a few weeks in Egypt. We would visit Cairo, the Great Pyramids, and the Valley of the Kings.

We left the kibbutz by foot, and then took a bus from Beit She'an to Jerusalem, of biblical fame. There we slept in a youth hostel and walked in the Old City market, a maze of alleys and stalls selling a bit of almost everything one could think of, but mostly a lot of carpets and brass teapots. We retraced part of the path supposedly taken by Jesus Christ when he carried the cross to the hill.

We took another bus southeast toward the city of Eilat, passing the Dead Sea, the lowest place on Earth at 1,400 feet below sea level. Growing up I had seen photos of my father swimming in the Dead Sea before I was born, buoyed above the water by the extreme salinity. Opposite the Dead Sea was a range of mountain plateaus. On one stood Masada, the historic fortress of Jewish freedom fighters who had struggled against Roman colonial rule. I had read a novel chronicling the siege of Masada, which happened in the year 73 CE. In this epic battle, 960 Jewish resistance fighters held out against 15,000 Roman troops for four months. When the Romans finally breached the walls, the Jewish rebels committed mass suicide instead of submitting to defeat and servitude. I looked up at the mountain where Masada's ruins lay and imagined how it might have looked almost 2,000 years ago, with massive ramparts and siege towers.

The next day we entered Egypt and the Sinai desert. As we rode down the Red Sea coast, the deep blue water contrasted with red desert mountains. The colors and topography were much more dramatic than anything I had seen in Israel. And it wasn't just the landscape that was different. The buses were old and worn, not new and clean like in Israel. People's features were different, and they spoke Arabic instead of Hebrew and English. Men wore long robes and kaffiyeh headdresses, and women wore hijab head scarves. Along the rough highway, there was less development and more roadside refuse, including countless plastic water bottles.

We reached Sharm El Sheikh, a Bedouin settlement and tourist village near the Sinai Peninsula's southernmost point. At that time it was a small collection of primitive structures, squat houses made of stone and tile. We followed signs advertising food and rooms for rent and found a handful of meager establishments. After sleeping in tiny quarters with dirt floors, we awoke the next day and continued on our way.

After a day traveling up the Peninsula's west coast, we took an all-night bus ride to Cairo. In the black of night, we knew we were crossing the Suez Canal but could not see it. When we arrived in Cairo early in the morning, we were let off near the city center in massive Tahrir Square. Decades later this site would be the birthplace of the Egyptian Revolution and part of the Arab Spring. The air was thick with pollution, and the square teemed with thousands of people. A small horde of children crowded around us. Dressed in little more than rags and extending open hands, they insistently begged for baksheesh, money.

From our hotel room window, the city seemed to stretch on forever into the smoggy horizon. At dusk, prayer chants broadcasted from mosques, a new sound for us, but it would soon become familiar. The next day we cautiously explored the city, including the many plazas and bazaars in our area. We continued to attract large groups of begging children. We gave money a few times but learned this created such a frenzied rush it was a bad idea.

Cafés lined the crowded streets. Most were full of local men smoking from hookahs. A couple of guys beckoned to us, and we accepted their invitation. All the men in the café were eager to meet us foreigners, and they crowded around us trying out the few English phrases they knew. Proud of their culture, they pressed the hookah on us. We passed the nozzle around and smoked sweetened tobacco. As we smoked they refilled the bowl, lit with smoldering embers. I had never smoked tobacco before, and I became dizzy, then nauseous. I ran out to the street and vomited. Some of the Egyptian men chuckled.

The next day we visited the ancient Pyramids of Giza. As our taxi approached the edge of the city, the pyramids grew before us. A mile away, they looked like small mountains. As we covered the final distance on foot, their enormity crystallized. Their individual blocks, which looked like bricks from a distance, were each the size of a small automobile. Wandering the grounds around the mountainous tombs, we saw the Great Sphinx with its noseless face and many other ruins.

*At the Great Pyramids of Giza, me on the right, Egypt, 1989.*

We signed on for a camel ride and a tour inside the Great Pyramid. Entering the pyramid through a gap between gargantuan stones, we descended into dark passages. Row upon row of hieroglyphics lined the walls. The air was still, and I sensed the pyramid's weight above us. We reached the Grand Chamber and the King's Chamber, the tomb of an ancient pharaoh. A god-king had been buried here, along with fabulous treasure. Thousands of years before, a massive slave-labor force had built a mountain to house this room. We left the pyramids, all three of us silent and contemplative, awestruck by the sole original remains of the Seven Wonders of the Ancient World.

*Eugene, Albert, and me (age 18) sitting on a pyramid.*

After two more days in Cairo, we took a southward bus to the city of Luxor and the nearby Valley of the Kings. We passed through familiar desert landscape, then entered the Nile River valley. The wide body of water streamed past us, and on either side was a narrow strip of lush, green cropland. Small villages occasionally interrupted the farmland with groups of low buildings the same color as the nearby sand. Traditional Egyptian felucca sailboats slowly glided across the water. High bluffs bordered either side of the river valley, buffering it from the wind and the ever-encroaching desert. The government had advised tourists to stay away from this region. There was an uprising of fundamentalist rebels at this time, and there had been bombings and shootings. We noticed as we went south there were less Westerners besides us.

After a long day on the bus we reached Luxor, a seat of power in the time of the Pharaohs. Right in the middle of town were the fantastic ruins of the Temple of Karnak. Massive stone pillars and crumbling walls dominated the skyline. The ruins were open for anyone to walk through, but we were tired and conducted only a quick survey before checking into a budget hotel.

The next morning we set out early, our sights set on reaching the legendary Valley of the Kings, burial ground of emperors. Catching a ferry across the Nile, Albert, Eugene, and I talked about how cool it was to be on this famous body of water.

We took a bus from the pier, then continued by foot on a dirt road through desert hills. Only a few cars passed us, and we saw just a handful of other people walking along the way. First we came to the Mortuary Temple of Queen Hatshepsut. This magnificent structure was carved into the base wall of a great cliff. As with the Pyramids, the Mortuary Temple's size was deceptive as we approached. The many pillars of the colonnaded terraces appeared small in comparison to the looming cliff. But when we got to the first terrace, each pillar was a small tower. Massive stone ramps joined the terraces, which we made our way up.

*That's me climbing on the ruins of old Luxor.*

Behind the colonnades, giant stone sarcophagi stood as they had since a distant age. Statues of bizarre beasts guarded, mostly headless. We were the only people there. At this time archeological treasures were loosely regulated in Egypt. Gleeful and ignorant, we climbed all over the ruins. Hopefully we didn't cause any damage. Eight years later, religious extremists would massacre sixty-two people at this exact place.

*Mortuary Temple of Queen Hatshepsut, Eugene and I walking.*

The Mortuary Temple was complex, and we could have spent the whole day exploring its mysteries, but we continued toward the Valley of the Kings. After a short hike we reached the valley, a depression surrounded by low desert hills. I was struck by the landscape's extreme bareness. There were no signs of moisture or vegetation anywhere, just sand and rock. It seemed a fitting location for tombs. The only person we saw was a lone guard in a ramshackle booth, and we toured the subterranean passages alone. The walls presented an endless mosaic of hieroglyphics and pictographs, which we could only wish to understand.

A European man on the ferry had suggested we visit a place called Deir el-Medina, the ruins of a village where the tomb builders had lived. In ancient Egypt, the people who worked on the kings' tombs had been forbidden contact with the rest of society. They had a town of their own out in the desert, isolated and heavily guarded. The site was a few kilometers from the Valley of the Kings, and we set out to find it.

There were no means of public transport, taxis, or anything much out there, so Eugene, Albert, and I continued to Deir el-Medina on foot, on dirt roads through hills. As we rounded a bend we saw what looked like one hundred or so crumbling stone structures. There were no modern buildings and no signs of a government presence or any other facilities. We were the only people there except for two Egyptian men who apparently were docents. They spoke a little broken English, managing to explain that the ruins were their responsibility and offering to show us around. As we entered the remains of the ancient town, it was clear the place had received little attention since being uncovered from the sand. There had been no improvements and no additions. There were just stone buildings protruding from the sand where they had been abandoned thousands of years before.

After showing us a few nondescript structures, the guides led us into a building larger than the others. They explained this was the house of a primary architect of the Valley of the Kings. The family had been quite well-off despite the social isolation. Entering a domed great room, we looked up to see an amazingly well-preserved mosaic still displaying its original design despite being more than 1,000 years old. It depicted a large fruit tree with roots delving into the earth and branches covered with green leaves. On one low branch hung a bright red fruit, and a serpent descended the gnarled trunk. A lion, holding a flaming sword, approached the tree. The serpent and lion faced each other with animosity, preparing for battle.

As we neared the end of our tour, our guides exchanged glances and said they had one more thing to show us. Shuffling their feet and looking around furtively, they indicated it wasn't part of the official tour and asked us not to talk to other people about it. Our curiosity was piqued, and we assured them we would keep quiet. They suggested we offer an additional contribution of baksheesh. Having become accustomed to Egyptian ways, my Irish friends and I expected no less and produced a suitable payment.

Our guides led us behind a group of buildings to an obscure corner of the ruins out of sight from the main road. We worried they might be setting us up for a robbery. When we reached a hole in the ground, they indicated this was our destination.

The hole was just large enough for one person to crawl into, and we waited nervously as one of the men disappeared into the hole. He reemerged dragging a large object in a burlap sack. As he removed the sack from his prize, our jaws dropped. To our amazement and revulsion, the mummified remains of a human being lay on the ground before us.

After recoiling in shock, we inched forward, fascinated. Moving close enough to touch it, we had a good look at the mummy. The cloth wraps were mostly disintegrated, and the legs were gone. The bones and a few shreds of skin seemed to be petrified. We could make out some facial features, the preserved, grey-brown skin stretched tightly over cheekbones. Some of the teeth were still in place, and they jutted out along with the jaw. Dark hollows stared from sockets where eyeballs used to be. The chest cavity was mostly empty. Shreds of muscle tissue resembled dusty beef jerky. Stone-like ribs, spine, shoulder girdle, and hips hung together. It was clearly ancient. Eugene furtively snapped a shot of it with his camera.

*The Egyptian docent and the mummy.*

The guides explained they had found the mummy in the ruins and had kept it hidden from authorities to make a little income, so would we please not mention it to anyone? We assured them we wouldn't and awkwardly thanked them for showing us their secret treasures.

As we walked back toward the Valley of the Kings, we discussed our amazing experience. It was surreal to have been close enough to an actual mummy to reach out and touch it. Seeing the still discernible features of a person who had lived thousands of years ago was disconcerting. I should have felt guilty about the exploitation of antiquities, but I didn't know better.

After that we backtracked north along the Nile to Cairo, then took a bus through the Sinai to Sharm El Sheikh. Eugene and Albert wanted to stay and vacation for another week, but my money was almost gone, so I continued on to Israel and the kibbutz. We said our goodbyes, sad to see our fellowship end. They gave me Albert's Walkman music player and a cassette tape of an Irish group called the Waterboys, which was my first introduction to Celtic music.

I caught a bus to the border. At the Israeli security checkpoint soldiers kept me in a room for several hours, questioning me occasionally. Eventually they evidently concluded that I posed no threat and released me.

At Eilat, I didn't have enough money for a hostel, so I spent the night on the beach. I curled up on a recliner chair and tried to stay warm. This was the only time on the trip that I used my leather motorcycle jacket. The next day I took a series of buses back to Beit She'an and started walking back to the kibbutz through the familiar fields.

As I walked, I passed an irrigation ditch flowing with clear water. There was a fenced area with a group of trees and some lush grass around the water, forming a kind of oasis in the arid farmland. Three Israeli teenage boys, one about my age and two slightly younger, were lounging in the shade and taking dips in the water. They called out to me. Although they didn't speak much English, and I almost no Hebrew, I understood they were inviting me to join them. Jumping the fence with my backpack, I took them up on the offer.

After cooling off in the water, we sat on the grass and attempted conversation. Indicating that I had recently come from Egypt, I took out some trinkets I had bought there as gifts and passed them around to show the boys. As the objects came back to me, I noticed a small bottle of perfume I had bought for my mother had disappeared. Believing it to be a mistake or a joke, I smiled and asked for it back. The boys feigned ignorance.

After repeated pleas, I stood up and demanded the perfume. They jumped to their feet and made it clear they were keeping it. I stepped toward them, unsure what to do but unwilling to accept the loss. The oldest boy grabbed a large bottle from the ground and smashed off the bottom on a rock. Advancing, he threatened me with the sharp glass. Jumping back, I looked around for a weapon and grabbed a large branch from the ground. A kind of rage came over me, and I went at the boys. I knocked the broken bottle from the boy's hand with the club and menaced all three, swinging the club over my head. Startled, they backed up.

At this point, maybe surprised by my challenge, they suddenly turned and ran. They jumped the fence and ran down a dirt road through the fields. For a moment I stood where I was, thinking I would let them go. Then I remembered the perfume. Determined not to let them get away with this injustice, I jumped the fence and chased them.

The boys had a head start and were a ways up the road. But I had run track in high school and was prepared to continue the pursuit as long as it took. After most of a mile, they began to slow, and I started to gain on them. The youngest of them was falling behind the others, and I finally overtook him. I grabbed him and dragged him to the ground, both of us tumbling in the dust. Straddling him, I held him down and gave him a good shake while calling out to the others. They looked around. Seeing their companion's plight, they stopped running.

I made like their friend was going to pay a dear price if they left with my perfume, threatening with my fist in the air. To their credit, the two came back to retrieve their comrade. I dragged the boy to his feet, holding him securely by his shirt collar. I motioned to the others I wanted a trade, their friend for my perfume. Finally, the oldest teenager produced the perfume, and we made the exchange. Walking back to the irrigation ditch, I recovered my pack and continued on to the kibbutz, satisfied justice had been done.

I spent my last couple weeks in Israel on or around the kibbutz. I pruned and tended avocado and citrus trees in the orchards, starting at 4:00 a.m. to beat the afternoon heat, and joined the volunteers in a trip to the nearby Jordan River. I had been looking forward to visiting this famous waterway. However, having experienced the pristine and gushing rivers of the Sierra Nevada, the Jordan seemed like a muddy creek.

It had been three months since my arrival, and my money was gone, so I prepared to return to California. I used my last $20 to reach the Tel Aviv airport and buy a snack before I boarded my plane to San Francisco.

# CHAPTER FOUR

# Mexico

In a hushed tone, Marcos said, "We are here."

Looking up, I saw we approached a clearing. While many of the ridges and ravines of this mountainous part of Oaxaca were arid and grassy, this north-facing area was more like a temperate rainforest. The path we had walked on for the past hour had gone through tall trees and thick undergrowth. Our footsteps and an occasional bird call were the only sounds, as we didn't talk.

Marcos was a Cuban expatriate we had met back in Zipolite, on the coast. I was with my high school friends Jim and Erica. Together we had hitchhiked 2,000 miles from San Francisco to this southern state of Mexico. Marcos had guided us to the remote village we had just arrived in, and now to visit a Native American shaman in the nearby mountains. We had reached our destination: the shaman's abode.

Tall trees gave way to willowy grass as we entered the clearing. Wisps of mist filtered through the surrounding canopy, and clouds obscured the sun. Birdcalls had ceased, and a deathly silence hung over the place. In the center of the clearing stood a ramshackle hut, elevated on rickety stilts.

The hut was made from random lumber, bits and pieces bound together at odd angles. I began to have second thoughts about this venture. We were in the middle of nowhere in Mexico with a man we barely knew, about to meet with a supposed witch doctor. What are we doing? I was about to suggest we turn back when Marcos broke the silence.

"*Hola!*" he called out.

We heard a thud from inside the hut. Marcos called out again, and after a moment what appeared to be a shambling heap of rags emerged. As we approached, I made out a wizened old lady bundled in robes. One eye wandered skyward as the other peered intently at us. Countless lines creased her leathery, aged face. A hump protruded from her back, and she walked with a limp.

Eyeing us suspiciously, the woman gruffly acknowledged Marcos, muttering a few words to him. Maybe she was asking who we were. After a brief conversation in Spanish, the shaman returned to her abode. Marcos followed and beckoned us to come along.

Putting doubt aside, we climbed the rickety stairs, stepped through a low doorway, and entered a tiny, dimly lit room. After a few minutes my eyes adjusted to the darkness, and I saw something like an altar, lit by an assortment of candles and decorated with statues, animal skulls, and other small objects. Scarves, beads, animal bones, and other items adorned the walls. The home's hunched-over resident bustled about, gathering small objects from drawers and containers while mumbling to herself.

Marcos guided us to sit on a small bench opposite the altar. The shaman placed objects on the altar and gathered ingredients into a mortar-like bowl. We waited a long time, occasionally glancing anxiously at Marcos, who motioned for us to remain still. Finally the witch doctor finished her tasks and turned suddenly toward us. She spoke in Spanish to Marcos, her voice rasping and cackling, and he translated. "Why are you here?"

Jim spoke. "We are here for a spiritual cleansing."

"What are you looking for?"

This time Erica volunteered. "Understanding."

The shaman grunted skeptically. "Why should I help you?"

Marcos replied before we could say anything, then indicated to us it was time for payment. We pulled out small bills and handed them to Marcos, who placed them on a side table. The shaman snatched up the wad and stuffed it into her robes, then resumed her preparations for we knew not what.

After a few minutes, she began chanting. She lit a bundle of incense and waved it in an intricate pattern along the walls and ceiling. Then she passed it over each of us, bathing us in smoke. The air grew thick, the light dimmer. My head was heavy, my thoughts slow and confused. The candle flames kept pulling at my gaze, and they seemed to grow larger as I listened to the hypnotic chanting. My awareness of the outside world disappeared.

Suddenly she stopped chanting and froze. Utter quiet permeated the room, and no one moved. After a few eerie moments she spun toward us and fixed a baleful glare on Jim. He shifted uncomfortably as she approached and motioned for him to stand up. When he stood to face her, Marcos translated her words. "What are you most afraid of?"

After a moment's hesitation, Jim answered. "Not finding a career."

The old woman grunted and took up her bundle of incense again. Making arcane gestures and resuming her chanting, she bathed Jim in smoke, then motioned for him to sit.

Next it was Erica, who stood up without hesitation. When asked the same question, Erica replied, "Being alone." The shaman went through the same smoke-bath ritual with her.

I stood up tentatively. The shaman peered into my face with one watery eye, and I struggled to hold her gaze. When asked about my fear, I was momentarily at a loss. Finally something came to me. "Mediocrity."

The shaman leaned in close and looked deeply into one of my eyes. Then she nodded, accepting my answer. She did the smoke-bath routine and released me to sit, which I did with relief.

The medicine woman carried out a few more rituals, blessing our group. She instructed us to avoid drugs, alcohol, and sex for the next three days, then abruptly indicated our session was at an end.

Uncomprehending, we remained still until Marcos prodded us up and out the door. Stumbling down the stairs, we awkwardly bade goodbye to the shaman, who ignored us.

We walked silently down the mountain path, each deep in our own thoughts. By the time we reached the village, we were exhausted and promptly went to sleep at our hotel.

After returning from Israel and Egypt, I stayed with my sister Mora and nephew Ryan back in Nevada County for the rest of the summer of 1989. Mostly I hung out on the Yuba River and did odd jobs for money. That winter I worked at Sugar Bowl ski resort in the Sierra Nevada Mountains near Lake Tahoe. It was just menial labor like shoveling snow and cleaning the lodge, but the snowboarding was amazing. Carving up steep alpine terrain was probably the most fun and athletic thing I had done by this point.

By spring I had saved $500 for another trip. My high school friends Erica and Jim were also looking for adventure.

Erica was a kindred free spirit and fearless when it came to world travel. Jim was a sincere, understated intellectual and a fellow fan of road trip literature. Together we decided to hitchhike through California and into Mexico. That was all we could afford, and it sounded good to us. We would make our way down Mexico's west coast as far as our meager funds allowed and return by an undetermined route.

I still had the military surplus backpack I had taken to Israel but added a wool blanket and Swiss Army knife to my gear and dropped the motorcycle jacket. Jim and Erica had similar packs. We each had about the same amount of money, which we carried as cash and traveler's checks. We had maps of California and Mexico, a copy of *The People's Guide to Mexico*, and our thumbs to catch rides.

We began our trip in mid-April, catching a ride to a freeway onramp on Highway 101 in San Francisco. The three of us stood there on the shoulder with our thumbs extended. It took a while, but eventually we hitched a ride, and then another and another. By midday we were in Santa Cruz, near some train tracks. We had read about riding freight trains across the U.S. and decided this was our chance to live that dream. We walked for two hours along the tracks, but a train never came. We abandoned our plan, almost certainly for the best as we could have been maimed or killed. We made our way to a freeway onramp and continued hitchhiking. By evening we arrived in Monterey, where we slept on the floor at a friend's house.

We hitchhiked south on Highway 1, which follows California's rugged coast all the way into Mexico. The two-lane road hugged steep cliffs facing the Pacific Ocean, passed over deep ravines, and plunged through mountain tunnels. It took several rides and a whole day to reach Los Angeles, where our last driver of the day said we could spend the night at his house. The guy was creepy, and we left before dawn the next morning.

Los Angeles freeways were unfriendly to hitchhikers, so we took a bus to San Diego and another to the border. We crossed into Mexico on foot and entered Tijuana. After walking for a couple of hours we found the youth hostel in our guidebook. We left early the next day to resume hitchhiking down Highway 1, which continues in Mexico to the southernmost point of the Baja California Peninsula.

We spent the next three days hitching rides south along Baja. The first night, we slept on the beach near Ensenada. At dawn we woke to find that during the night, the tide had brought sewage from the nearby town within a few feet of where we were sleeping. Fortunately the foul tide had missed us, but we also discovered that someone had gone through our bags. Various small items were gone. This did not include our money and essential documents, which we kept on our bodies when we slept. My disposable camera was gone, which is why I have no photos from this trip. This was a wakeup call, and we learned to be more careful and alert.

Baja California is mostly arid desert, vast tracts of land with little more than scrub brush and cacti. Highway 1 runs north to south as it does in the U.S., but midway down the peninsula it cuts across to the east coast, where it continues along the Sea of Cortez. Towns are few and far between, especially in the midsection. On the second night we splurged on a hotel room because we couldn't find anywhere appropriate or secure to camp. The hotel was in a tiny village, just a few low, dusty buildings on the dry plain.

The next day, though there wasn't much traffic, we caught several good rides without having to wait long. Soon we were approaching the small city of La Paz near the southernmost tip of the peninsula. We walked to the seashore to find a place to camp. There was nothing except a rocky beach, the Sea of Cortez's quietly splashing surf, and a tiny abandoned hut probably used by fishermen. We were the only people in sight and it was getting dark, so we decided to rest in the hut.

The hut had three walls and a roof. It sat directly over the rocks, with the open side facing the water. Inside hung a ragged hammock. The hammock stood up to our weight-bearing tests, and we decided Erica would sleep in it. Jim and I settled onto the rocks. Each of us had only a single blanket as bedding and our bags as pillows, and we struggled to get comfortable. We grew quiet as a full moon rose over the sea and small waves broke against the shore a few feet from us. City lights sparkled down the coast, but here there was only quiet and nature. I watched the moon's reflection on the water and fell asleep.

In the morning we shook the stiffness from our bodies and walked the last few kilometers to La Paz on a dusty road. We rented a hotel room in the city center, showered, and explored the charming town. We visited markets, churches, and the seaside promenade. The next day we boarded a ferry bound for Mazatlán on the Mexican mainland. Dolphins swam along beside our ship.

Mazatlán was bigger than any community we had passed since Tijuana and had the hustle and bustle of a tourism hub and port city. We didn't stop there, continuing to hitchhike south on the coastal highway. That night we hopped a fence in the dark to camp in an open field. When we woke with the dawn, we found ourselves surrounded by cattle. Swiftly gathering our things, we fled the pasture as an immense bull eyed us angrily.

We arrived in Puerto Vallarta, another midsize coastal town and tourist destination. On a pleasant beach, we found a spot sheltered between some trees and decided to camp there. Before setting camp we went to a nearby market and bought refried beans, fresh tortillas, and mangos. With no cooking equipment or utensils other than pocketknives, we ate mostly simple, raw foods, usually straight from the can or bag.

Various rides took us slowly down the Pacific coast, with truckers or families, in the backs of pickups, and once with an American surfer in an old VW bus. We slept on beaches and fields, doing our best to avoid attention. Finally we came to the state of Oaxaca, and the southernmost point of the coast before it bends to the northeast. We had hitchhiked more than 2,500 miles.

In the small town of Puerto Angel, we heard about cheap lodging a few kilometers away at a beach called Zipolite. There we found a gorgeous white sand beach tucked between two hills. Rolling breakers churned the water, and restaurants and hostels lined the road above the beach, some renting hammocks for a few dollars per night. We decided to rest at this budget traveler's Mecca and spent the next several days there, playing in the ocean surf and lounging on the hot sand. In the evenings we lay in our hammocks and discussed travel, politics, and history with travelers from around the world. This was where we met Marcos, a veteran traveler exiled from his native Cuba for we knew not what. He impressed us with his many entertaining stories, and when he invited us to join him on a visit to a remote Native American village, we jumped at the chance.

After the visit to the shaman, we said our farewells to Marcos. We knew in all likelihood we would never see him again and sincerely thanked him for guiding us to places and experiences we would always remember. We climbed into the village's lone taxi, which would take us to the main highway. Marcos waved and called out a final "*Adios!*"

We waited on the highway for an hour before catching a bus heading north. We were bound for Oaxaca City, our final major destination. After several transfers in mountain villages, we crested a summit and caught sight of the city. Nestled in a beautiful high mountain valley, the city was surrounded by peaks and ranges. From afar we saw many green parks and church spires. The air was cool and clear, and sun rays beamed down through billowing clouds. To our eyes, Oaxaca City was a magical sight, and we entered the city charmed.

We stepped off the bus at the *zócalo*, the main square at the city center. Colonnaded buildings and stone arches surrounded this large plaza, and tree-lined walkways led to an elaborate gazebo and fountains at the center. The zócalo was full of people. Vendors sold churros and other food and beverages.

At one of the many cantinas bordering the zócalo, we ordered tamales and beer and settled down to consider our options. Soon a man who appeared to be the restaurant owner approached our table. With a friendly smile, he spoke to us in Spanish. *"Señores y señorita, buenas tardes!"*

*"Buenas tardes,"* we responded, always happy to employ what minimal Spanish we had.

*" ¿Son de los Estados Unidos?"* he queried.

*"Sí,"* we replied.

*"Bienvenidos a Oaxaca!"* He boomed. *"Una pregunta: ya ha probado nuestro mezcal?"*

This complex question baffled me and Jim, so we turned to Erica. Of the three of us, her Spanish was the best. "He asked if we've tried the local mescal liquor."

We replied that we had not, and the kindly man smiled and disappeared into the kitchen. Returning with a tray with three small glasses of liquor, he set them down on our table with an air of triumph. *"Este es el mezcal de Oaxaca!"* he said with pride.

Surprised by the alcohol and generosity, we paused as the man waited expectantly. We raised the glasses to our host and downed the fiery liquor. Smooth to the taste, the mescal sent a rush of warmth into my chest. We smiled and nodded enthusiastically. *"Gracias!"*

"*¿Es bueno, no?*" he asked.

"*Sí, muy bueno!*"

The man laughed and returned to work. We agreed that one good turn deserved another and ordered another round of mescal shots for ourselves and the owner. Soon we were pretty buzzed and realized we should move on and find a place to stay before things got out of hand. We asked the generous restaurateur for a suggestion for a cheap hotel and followed his directions around the corner to a small side street. Here we found the tiny posada run by a family who lived there. We settled in, tired after a long day of travel and drinking.

The next day was May 5, a Mexican national holiday. As we explored the neighborhoods surrounding the zócalo, we noted many colorful decorations on the picturesque buildings. Oaxaca City impressed us with its charm and beauty. It was the most attractive town we visited in our travels in Mexico, full of graceful architecture, grand churches, lush parks, and busy plazas. The main streets were wide and clean. Quaint restaurants, art studios, and shops populated numerous alleys and side lanes. Many of the buildings, fountains, and statues were made from a local green stone, which enhanced the city's verdant appearance.

Homes and restaurants buzzed with cooking, preparatory sounds—the city was preparing for a fiesta. We wandered until midday, then made our way back toward the zócalo and our posada.

When we turned onto our street, we met with a surprising sight: a parade of fantastically costumed individuals headed in our direction. They were probably no more than one hundred people, but they were loud and animated and filled the street. Some played a cacophonous tune on drums and horns while others danced wildly, hugged each other, or whooped in joy.

Somebody in the merry, raucous group saw us and shouted, directing everyone's attention our way. Apparently the sight of three gringos was cause for celebration, or perhaps rage. We did not know which as the whole group let out a mighty yell and began running straight at us.

Unsure about a course of action, we looked at each other. "Should we run away?" I asked.

"Maybe we should duck into the posada real quick before they get to us," Erica suggested.

Jim wanted to take a chance. "Let's join them and see what happens."

Swallowing our fears, we agreed with Jim and braced ourselves. The unruly parade crashed on us like a wave, enveloping us in people. At first it seemed like our fears might be realized as the revelers grabbed us and swept us along. We relaxed when we realized they just wanted us to dance and join them in celebration.

Upon closer look, we saw that most of the partiers were young men dressed in drag or elaborate animal costumes. They swung us into a wild waltz, spinning us through the crowd as others danced and twirled around us. We went along, laughing and dancing crazily, careful to keep each other in sight.

The Oaxacans passed us from person to person, taking turns dancing with us. Then a new faction of the bacchanalian mob got to us with a joyous roar: the hard-drinking crowd. They were quick to press us into action. One of them grabbed me and tipped back my head as another held a massive pitcher to my lips. Some kind of tequila punch gushed into my mouth. I did my best to swallow it as excess streamed down my neck and chest. I saw Jim and Erica in similar positions. At every turn, people passed us another drink as we danced madly through the streets.

Soon we were far from our posada and falling toward the back of the parade. The group seemed to lose interest in us and left us behind. Looking about in bewilderment, we laughed and swayed as they disappeared around a corner. We calmed down, our laughter quieting, and for a moment we simply stood giggling in the middle of the street, drunk again. We found our way back to the posada, rested, and spent the evening at the zócalo observing the Cinco de Mayo festivities. They were fun and colorful, but nothing came close in pure zealous revelry to that small neighborhood parade.

Our funds were nearly spent—it was time to head back to the United States. We caught a bus to Mexico City. Unfortunately we could not spend much time in this remarkable metropolis, as we were racing home before all our money ran out. We thought it would be cheaper in the end to catch a train through Mexico than to hitchhike. Though hitchhiking is free, it takes much longer, and during that time one must eat, find places to stay, etcetera. At the central station in Mexico City, we boarded a train bound for Mexicali on the U.S. border. We rode the train for two long days, cramped in the crowded economy section. We slept in our seats as dusty landscapes passed by. Finally we arrived in Mexicali and crossed the border on foot.

We resumed hitchhiking in California's arid southeast corner. As was often the case, we waited a long time before someone gave us a ride. We rode through agricultural land, then a harsh, rocky desert. Eager for more hospitable climates, we didn't stop until we reached Irvine, where we slept on a lawn on the University of California campus.

It took two more days to hitchhike to San Francisco. We spent another night on a college campus, this time on a sports field in San Louis Obispo. The ocean was nearby, and the marine layer made it too cold to get much sleep. At dawn we awoke from fitful rest to find an armadillo nosing around our camp. Before we could react, the sprinklers came on and the armadillo disappeared. We grabbed our bags and ran off the field dodging jets of water.

At the nearest freeway on-ramp, a matte black van, battered and worn, pulled up. The side door opened and two straggly-haired rockers beckoned us in. It looked sketchy, but as they say, beggars can't be choosers. The young couple seemed strung out but were friendly and nice. They had driven from New Jersey to California in search of a new life. This turned out to be the final ride of our hitchhiking odyssey, as they were going to San Francisco.

Our voyage was at an end. The three of us walked to a bus station, realizing that from here we would go our separate ways. The whole trip had taken only one month, but it seemed much longer. As we waited for our buses to arrive we settled into a melancholy quiet, unsure what to say. It was sad to see our grand adventure end. We had been through so much together. It had been a journey we would remember forever, and I sensed we would never do anything like it again. We embraced each other as Jim's bus arrived, and Erica and I watched with moist eyes as it rumbled away.

CHAPTER FIVE

# Vision Quest

A fter Mexico, I took another job in the Sierra Nevada mountains, this time at a place called the Cedars. The Cedars is a few thousand acres of forested land along with a few dozen cabins and a clubhouse. Owned by an association of old-money families, it comprises the headwaters basin of the North Fork of the American River, a high mountain valley ringed by snowy peaks. The area is lush in the spring and summer, with gushing streams, cascading waterfalls, and plentiful wildlife. Several of my buddies and I were part of the early crew, arriving while there was still snow on the ground. It was our job to open the cabins by removing shutters, installing awnings, repairing plumbing, and cleaning up after bear break-ins. We also cleared a lot of brush and fallen trees. The crew lived in one big single-room cabin. Our boss Jim was an angular and weather-worn mountain man, well versed in local lore. When we weren't working, we hiked to mountain tops, swam in icy streams, and drank the beer Jim occasionally gave us as a bonus.

I read somewhere about young Native Americans in the old days sent into the wilderness on vision quests, to be tested and gain enlightenment. I admired rites of passage like this from other ages and cultures. I imagined that persevering through challenges, journeys, and quests forged youths into strong adults, competent and confident.

I felt that our culture, or at least my life, lacked sufficient rites of passage like this. So I tried to create voyages or situations that would test my mettle and skills. And, I decided to set up my own version of a vision quest.

The plan was to get dropped off about ten miles into the nearby wilderness. After camping out for one night, I would then hike along the river back to the Cedars. Ten miles isn't such a long hike, but it would be in the steep and rugged terrain of the Royal Gorge. This is the massive canyon carved out by the American River as it is squeezed between two converging mountain ridges. Jim warned me it was rough country and would be difficult to get through on foot. And I wasn't bringing any food, so it would be a fast. I did have some psilocybin mushrooms, though. One of the guys had given me them to help me on my quest.

I had two days off, and asked Jim to drive me up the four-wheel-drive road to Wabena Ridge. The ridge overlooks the massive Royal Gorge, formed by Snow Mountain on the north side and Wabena Ridge on the south. At the bottom of the Gorge lies the North Fork of the American River, with rapids, granite slabs, and many waterfalls. I had a backpack, water, a tarp, a blanket, and the mushrooms. I would hike straight down into the Gorge and find Rattlesnake Falls, which I had been told were spectacular. Then I would camp out by the falls and take the mushrooms. The next day I would hike eight miles or so along the river back to the Cedars.

Jim drove me to the top of Wabena Ridge. Before he left, he showed me a big slab of granite near the ridge's point. On it there were strange forms carved into the stone: petroglyphs, symbols left by Native Americans hundreds of years before. I could guess some of the symbols' meanings. One image looked like a hand with six fingers. Two parallel wavy lines might have symbolized the rivers below. Or maybe they were snakes. Other strange shapes were completely indecipherable. All together there were about twenty carvings. The Neolithic people who created this mural had used only Stone Age tools. It must have taken many hours of hard work to carve these figures. But whatever the petroglyphs had meant to people who had stood at this exact spot many centuries before, now it was a mystery.

Jim pointed out an obscure trailhead, wished me luck, and reminded me I was expected at work in two days. I assured him I would be there and set out walking. Quickly descending into the canyon, I stopped to admire stunning views. To my left the great chasm stretched out and opened into the horizon. I stood on the Gorge's steep south wall, blanketed by coniferous forest. Directly across the Gorge, Snow Mountain dominated the north wall. A great mass of mostly bare rock, Snow Mountain dwarfed everything around it. From its summit it dropped a tremendous 4,000 feet to the river. Beneath its huge, gray-white dome, shimmering rivulets of snow runoff cascaded down the stony face. There was forest near the bottom, but higher up, the only vegetation was an occasional green dot, a solitary tree.

To my right the Gorge narrowed and split into several tributary canyons, forming a maze of mountainous waterways. Far below was the river, a white and blue ribbon winding through the Gorge's floor. On my trail, I noticed several surprisingly large bear scats. Wary of an unwanted encounter, I continued on my way.

The trail was steep but only about three miles from beginning to end. Before long I reached the bottom of the Gorge and the American River. Passing a Forest Service footbridge, I stayed on the river's south side and headed downstream. Hopping from one giant rock to another, I soon found Rattlesnake Falls. The descriptions I had heard were accurate—the falls were magnificent. After being forced through a narrow gap between two granite walls, the river waters shot out into the air and fell about sixty feet to the pool below. Halfway down the falls, a horizontal rock shelf jutted out from behind the waterfall, sending some of the water into a second arc before it hit the water below. A massive cloud of mist billowed off the thunderous cascade. The deep blue pool at the bottom was surrounded on three sides by sheer stone cliffs. From one of these cliffs I saw several trout swimming in the clear water. The loud roar, amplified by the natural rock bowl, blasted upward into my face and the open sky. I had arrived at my destination. I found a sandy flat a little ways from the falls and made my camp.

As far as I knew, there was nobody else in the Royal Gorge with me. There was wildlife in the area, though, including deer and bears. The wind rustled the pines, and chipmunks scurried on rocks.. The sound of the falls here fell to a deep murmur. I spread the tarp on the ground and sat down for a rest, ignoring my rumbling stomach. As per my plan, I had brought no food. I was eager to eat the mushrooms and commence whatever psychic journey they brought, but I also wanted to jump off those cliffs into the waterfall pool. It seemed unwise to mix the two, so I decided to jump in the water first.

The sun was still high when I reached the pool, and the water glistened with refracted light. I stood for a long while taking in the sight. So much water gushed through the air and fell with such power. To the side of the falls, a miniature cedar tree grew in a small nook in the cliff, lonely in its precarious position. About forty feet below me, the deep blue pool beckoned. I took off my shirt and shoes and gathered my courage for the jump. I was confident the pool was deep enough to land in safely, but the drop was long. I stepped to the cliff's edge. I had to do it quickly or I might not do it at all. I leapt.

It was such a brief moment in time, but so rich in sensation. First there was lunging into the air and leaving the safety of solid ground behind. Then rapid acceleration downward, gaining speed at an alarming but exhilarating rate. The pool's crystalline waters rushed toward me while ashen stone walls raced by. Trying to control my position in the air, I braced for impact. Slam! I hit the pool's rippled surface and shot deep under cold water. Opening my eyes I saw an aquamarine world full of rising bubbles. A fish swam by. I pushed to the surface and burst up, gasping for air. In an instant, it was done.

I laughed out loud, climbed back up the wall, and jumped again. Then I warmed myself by lying on the sun-heated granite. By this time the sun hung low in the sky, so I headed back to my campsite.

I made myself comfortable on my tarp and broke out the mushrooms—shriveled grey fungi in a small bag. I was nervous and unsure about the mushrooms. My goal of a vision quest was only half-serious. I knew I was in no position to have a real vision quest like the ones I had read about. Those included deep religious beliefs, elaborate ritual, and severe deprivation. But I was in search of adventure, and this would be a psychic adventure. I put the foul-smelling things in my mouth.

The taste was horrible. It was earthy in a bad way. I struggled not to gag and forced myself to chew. Finally I ground them up enough to swallow, and I gulped them down. Grateful to wash away the foul flavor, I drank some water. Then I sat on the tarp and admired the scenery while waiting for the mushrooms to take effect.

Thirty minutes passed and nothing happened. Then, faintly at first, I felt butterflies in my stomach and chest. Excitement and increased energy arose, along with a tinge of anxiety. My head felt light, and my thoughts grew detached and abstract. I had the urge to go running into the woods, but I stayed put.

The butterflies and anxiety increased. My thoughts raced, bouncing around among all manner of subjects. The sensations rose to a frenetic crescendo, then suddenly calmed down. The butterflies disappeared, and my body felt warm and still. My speeding mental stream slowed, and I looked up.

Colors were deeper and more vibrant than normal. Forest green, sky blue, the red-brown cedar tree bark, and even the granite rocks glowed. Geometric patterns emerged from the waving pine needles in the nearby forest's coniferous canopy. All of a sudden they were the most fascinating things in the world, and I stared as angular shapes materialized before my eyes. After a long moment, I tore away my gaze to see fractal patterns slowly emerge from a nearby rock surface. I looked closer as minuscule details crystallized. Tiny ridges in the rock stood out in stark relief, lichen colonies looked like forests, and geometric patterns formed and dissolved in a constant progression.

Each scene and object seemed alive with colors, textures, and patterns. After who knows how long, I became aware of another sense, one I had forgotten—sound. Suddenly I noticed the roar of the distant falls and the gurgling of the river where it bent closer to my position. There were rumbles, drips, and splashes, an endless, watery symphony. Then something much different, a sweet song rising above the water's din. It was a bird call echoing off the rock walls.

I stayed there a long time taking in all the visual and sonic stimulation. Then, hopping from rock to rock, I came into view of the mountain gorge that held me in its basin.

The granite capped ridges shimmered in the golden radiance of the setting sun. Shades of orange, red, and pink progressively took over the sky. Snow Mountain's shadow slowly grew to envelop first the river and then my camp. Everything looked like a magnificent, animated painting, and I was in awe. Full of wonder, I wandered around the area until the high slowly wore off.

Later, as I lay on my blanket to sleep, my mood became contemplative and serious. Despite the mushroom trip, my thoughts turned to finding a career. Shoestring travel and seasonal jobs were great and all, but really, what was I going to do? Actually, being in nature like this was great—maybe I could become a biologist or forester. But that seemed to me largely solitary work, and I had already spent too much time alone. Ah well, something will present itself, I thought, and let it go.

My mind turned to more pleasant subjects, and eventually came upon capoeira. Just a few months before I had encountered it for the first time. It was when I was visiting my mother and sisters Valerie and Erin in San Francisco. Erin had somehow discovered capoeira and had been practicing for a couple of years. One night she took me along with her to a class. I had no idea what to expect, but was instantly impressed.

The class was in a community center across the Bay in Oakland. When we entered the large, open space, the barrage of sounds and sights overwhelmed me for a moment. To one side people were playing a kind of music I had never heard before. Some students did impressive acrobatics on gymnastic mats while others practiced martial arts together, including kicks and takedowns. The dynamic movements joined with a kind of swinging, side-to-side step. It looked so smooth and graceful, yet dangerous.

At the end of class everyone formed a circle. On one side, people held the same strange instrument in their hands. A wooden bow about four feet long, it had a round resonator box attached near the bottom end. The box was made from a gourd, which was held against the belly of the musician with the length of the bow extending upward. This was the *berimbau*, the heart and soul of capoeira music.

The class hushed. One of the berimbaus was struck and it produced a twangy note. Then the others chimed in, and a drum began thumping. A singer called out a refrain, and the rest of the group answered with a loud chorus. I had never seen live music just spring into life like this. I didn't understand it much, but the hairs on the back of my neck rose, and my pulse quickened.

Two students shook hands and cartwheeled into the center. They kicked and dodged, their feet barely missing each other's heads. Throwing in spins and flips, they circled each other in a wild exchange of movement. I couldn't tell if it was sparring, dance, or competition. Afterwards I learned it was all of these. I was amazed and thought, I want to learn this!

Now, lying under the open sky in the Royal Gorge, I recalled the experience. At that time, capoeira was almost completely unknown in the United States. Barely anyone had heard of it, and there were only a handful of teachers in the whole United States. It was so novel, and unlike anything else I knew of. The people I had seen in class were a diverse group, something in itself I had rarely seen. They practiced acrobatics, martial arts, and music, and put it together in an interactive game. They were participating as a community in a authentic cultural art, something I had always wanted to do.

Suddenly it came to me: *capoeira!* That was the answer to my riddle. Capoeira could become my thing. Somehow I could have a career involving it. The vision was vague and unarticulated, but powerful. Somehow I knew from then on that capoeira would be a big part of my life. I decided then that after my gig at the Cedars I would head to the Bay Area and begin taking classes.

The next morning I woke with a clear head, sore back, and ravenous hunger. My stomach felt like an empty pit. I had to get back to the Cedars as soon as possible, so I washed my face in the river, packed my few things, and headed out.

Walking upstream from Rattlesnake Falls, I tread on a well-worn trail that followed the river, passing by small rapids and picturesque pools. I crossed the river on the Forest Service footbridge and passed Palisades Creek tumbling down a series of falls. At a fork in the trail, I took a right to stay near the American river.

For a couple of hundred yards the trail continued parallel to the river on a chaparral-covered hillside. Then it abruptly ended. There was no sign, turn, or other distinguishing feature, just a dead end facing a dense manzanita thicket. Jim's warning came to mind. This was where I would have to make my own trail. I commenced pushing through the manzanita. The bushes were thick and as high as my head, and for every branch I stepped on or pulled aside, another one pushed against my chest or scraped my bare arms and legs.

I descended to the river, hoping to rock-hop straight up from there. But when I arrived at the river's edge and looked upstream, I saw this was impossible. The river here was a mass of water passing between two cliffs, with no way to pass. I reluctantly climbed the hill again. This time I kept going past the manzanita. I climbed until the grade decreased and the inhospitable thicket gave way to pine forest. This was much more navigable, so I turned and walked parallel the river, high above on the ridge top.

I made good progress over fallen trees and tangled deadwood, but I was moving farther and farther from the river. Every time I tried to veer to the right and downhill, I encountered thick manzanita or cliffs too steep to pass. I knew eventually I would need to go back down the canyon or risk getting lost in the mountains. Finally I came upon a tributary stream that cut through the terrain. I followed the small waterway, which was beautiful in itself. Crystal clear spring water rolled and tumbled over rocks, between trees, and around small islands. Jumping from rock to rock I descended quickly, still ignoring my gnawing hunger.

There was a flash of movement ahead, and I slowed to approach carefully. Crawling between boulders and trees, I turned a corner and looked ahead. About thirty or forty yards downstream were a large black bear and smaller bear cub. I froze. I had been warned about a mama bear's ferocity while with cub. I was in danger and had to be careful about my next move. If I made a noise or even if the bear caught my scent, she could charge and maul me.

Luckily I was downwind from the bears, and they had not detected my presence. I stayed put, hidden by fallen trees, watching intently. The adult bear pawed and rummaged about, looking for food. The cub dutifully followed her around, curiously sniffing everything it came across. The cub was cute, and the mama bear beautiful in her own powerful way, but I knew better than to get any closer.

After a few minutes the bears headed downstream, the same way I was headed. I considered my options. I could leave the stream and climb the mountainside again, but this was a topographically complex area with many minor peaks and intersecting streams. If I became lost with no food and minimal camping gear, I could be in trouble. Backtracking to the trail and Rattlesnake Falls was not an option because there was no feasible way out from there. I could leave the stream bed and attempt to bypass the bears, beating them to the main river. If I did so, I risked surprising them and causing a potentially catastrophic encounter. So I followed the bears downstream toward the American River.

I needed to stay far enough away from the bears to remain undetected but close enough not to lose track of them. I would let them get out of my eyesight, then carefully creep forward, just close enough to see them again. They slowly continued downstream, pausing to investigate here and there as they went. I chose each step cautiously, careful not to break a twig or make any other sound.

After about an hour of this, I finally sighted the river through some trees. Relieved to see it again, I was especially happy because here the river looked shallow and wide. This meant there would probably be a level shoreline and boulders along the banks. Now I just had to get past the bears. I watched as they reached the river's edge and hoped they would not turn upstream. If they did, I would be in essentially the same situation I had been in for the past hour. Luckily, after a pause, they turned downstream and headed out of sight.

I made my way to where the stream met the river and looked around. Upstream the river was as I had suspected, wide and navigable. Downstream it was similar but bordered by steeper hillsides, narrowing as it descended. The bears were already a good distance downstream, walking away from me in some shallows. I knew this was a dead end and quickly headed upstream before they came this way again.

By this time it was early afternoon, and I was ravenous. It had been foolish not to bring food. Not for the first or last time, impulsiveness had gotten me in a jam. With a sense of urgency, I made my way up the river, jumping from rock to rock, pushing through bushes along the shore, and sometimes walking in the water. I kept this up for a couple of hours and covered maybe two miles or so. Then the canyon grew steep again. I scrambled and climbed.

I was beginning to worry I was approaching another impassible section when I heard a new sound. It was the distant roar of a large waterfall. There was only one other big waterfall between Rattlesnake Falls and the Cedars: Heath Falls. This massive cascade marked the border of the North Fork Association's land and the beginning of the trail to the Cedars.

Rounding a bend in the river, the falls came into view. Heath Falls is perhaps even more impressive than Rattlesnake. The water forms a single thick curtain as it drops over the edge of a sheer cliff, descending seventy feet in free fall to the pool below. The impact of the water hitting the pool creates a large cloud of mist that obscures the surface. The surrounding canyon is deep and narrow, preventing sunlight from reaching the bottom except at midday. I was below the falls and looked for a way to get above them. Luckily I was on the river's north side. The south side was a smooth stone wall impossible to scale, and the river was too deep to ford. In my area was a steep dirt hill dotted with bushes. It looked climbable, so I began the ascent.

I clawed my way up the hill, grabbing bushes and digging my fingers into the earth. Eventually I reached the top, covered in dirt. Walking along cliff tops toward the falls, I finally found the trail. Exhausted and relieved, I began the hike's final segment. I still had several miles to go, but it was on a well-worn trail I knew. Soon I would be back at the Cedars.

An hour later I arrived at our cabin, grateful and exhausted. My "vision quest" was complete. Not what I had romanticized about those of Native Americans, but also not so far off—the journey had been cathartic. It had been a test, and a valuable experience. And, now I knew my direction. I would go to the San Francisco Bay Area to learn capoeira.

# CHAPTER SIX

# Berkeley

"W hat do we want?"
"Peace!"
"When do we want it?"
"Now!" The crowd's thunderous reply met the clarion call of the bullhorn.

This was in downtown San Francisco in late 1990. The U.S. armed forces and its allies had just invaded Kuwait on the orders of President George W. Bush. As the first Gulf War began, our country went into an uproar, with frantic voices arguing for and against the conflict. Like most people in the Bay Area, I was against the war. It seemed like madness—a thinly veiled scheme for big business oil and weapon industry profit.

We heard about a big protest being organized in San Francisco, so some friends and I took the BART train there from Berkeley. Emerging from the underground train station onto the street, we met with a sea of protesters. Market Street was closed to auto traffic and filled with tens of thousands of people slowly marching toward the Federal Building. Protestors waved signs and banners urging peace, flags blew in the wind, drums pulsed, and from an upstairs window a powerful sound system blasted John Lennon's "Imagine" and "Give Peace A Chance."

The crowd arrived at the Federal Building and filled the square in front of it. The building had not opened yet. We strained to hear a protest leader who stood on top of a truck and spoke through a bullhorn. The crowd's objective was to keep employees out of the Federal Building by forming a human chain around it. Riot police would arrive soon. We were to hold together against them, remaining nonviolent at all costs. Two people demonstrated how to make a link with each other by locking arms at the elbows, and we spread out and created a chain around the building. There were so many of us we made two lines, concentric human circles, preparing ourselves for what may come.

There was the rumble of large vehicles and shouts of "They're here! The police are coming!" We closed our lines. Who knew how long our human barricade would hold out? But we were determined. The police came into sight, two rows of them in riot gear, marching in unison toward us. Their resolve was evident in their lockstep and icy stares. I felt afraid. I was vaguely aware of pain in my arms as the protestors' grips tightened on each other. The police were almost upon us. We braced ourselves, leaning forward against anticipated blows.

The police hit our line near me, thrusting riot shields against our intertwined bodies. In an instant they easily broke through both of our chains. I tumbled to the ground as they pushed protesters aside. They quickly and efficiently opened a corridor between the street and the Federal Building doors and lined it, ending our blockade. The police breached the barricade in multiple areas, and the protesters milled about, not knowing what to do. Government employees entered the building.

Just like that the protest was over, and the crowd dispersed. My friends and I caught a train back to the East

Bay. Back in Berkeley, life went on, and the war was over in a few months.

After the Cedars, I had hitchhiked from Donner Summit to the Bay Area. Rides were few and far between, and by nightfall I had only made it as far as Vacaville. I spent the night camped in a grove of eucalyptus trees. This time I huddled in a sleeping bag as a windstorm shook the canopy above.

The next day was the Fourth of July, and I hitched a ride all the way to Berkeley. I walked several miles from the freeway to the University of California. On campus there were a lot of people walking about, mostly in their twenties and thirties. The population was racially diverse, which was refreshing after the homogeneity of rural California. The campus had beautiful landscaping and architecture. The stately halls and air of studiousness piqued my intellectual curiosity. For the first time, I thought I might want to go to college.

I left campus and walked down Telegraph Avenue, which had an entirely different atmosphere. A wide array of restaurants, bookstores, music shops, and vintage clothing boutiques hemmed the boulevard. Vendor tables on the street sold jewelry, clothes, crafts, and other items. The sidewalks teemed with an eclectic mix including students, artists, musicians, tourists, and homeless people. The vibe felt leftwing, bohemian, beatnik, proletariat, hippie, rebellious. It was a kaleidoscope of culture, a holdover of the '60s and the Summer of Love with a flair all its own.

Erica lived in Berkeley at the time and said I could crash at her apartment for a few nights. I walked a few blocks from Telegraph Avenue to the address she had given me. Nobody was home, so I sat on the front lawn to wait. A man with a long white beard and tie-dyed Grateful Dead shirt stopped to chat with me. After a few minutes, he tossed me a joint and wished me a happy Fourth of July. Erica eventually showed up and let me into the apartment, where I rested and cleaned up.

It took me a few months to find my footing as I bounced around between places to live and restaurant jobs. Eventually I rented a room and found full-time work at the Bison Brewing Company brewpub. The Bison was an eclectic new establishment on Telegraph Avenue. It was one of the first of the microbreweries sprouting up on the West Coast and the hub of an urban tribe. A diverse, beer-loving family, we came from different backgrounds but found common ground in freewheeling Berkeley. The management was permissive and mostly hands-off. They let us be creative and keep the bar open after hours for extended partying. I was the youngest employee at nineteen, tending the bar even though I was not yet legal to drink. I became a kind of kid brother in the group. When they learned of my Irish heritage, the crew nicknamed me Paddy, which stuck for many years.

I upgraded my transportation from my trusty skateboard to a motorcycle. My first bike was a gray Kawasaki KZ 550. It was a good motorcycle, an early generation Japanese racing bike. It handled well, but it was heavy and needed a lot of repair. I kept it for about a year, then upgraded to a 1987 Yamaha FZ 600. This was one of the first modern sport-bikes, fast and nimble. It was already well used when I bought it, and it showed. It was missing some of the faring, the fiberglass outer body that gives sport and racing motorcycles their smooth, aerodynamic shape. The FZ also required regular maintenance—but it was a joy to ride, so responsive and fast. It would be my sole means of transportation for the next six years.

The motorcyclists at the Bison were diverse. Mathew was suave and cultured, on a super-fast GSXR 750. My old friend Ian had also moved to Berkeley and taken a job at the Bison. He rode a classic old BMW R100. Marvin and Tej were of

Japanese and Indian descent respectively, but both rode Kawasaki KZ1000s. I loved these bikes because they were the same model as those in the movie Mad Max. Dan was a college professor and had a rare Yamaha single cylinder motorcycle, and Susan on her newer BMW K model was one of the few female riders around. Paul was a blue collar rebel who also rode a BMW R100, and who took me under his wing to teach me motorcycle repair. Together we raced through the Berkeley hills, the streets of San Francisco, and on the costal highways. We were young, free, and a bit wild, careening around the state with joy and abandon.

A few months after moving to Berkeley, I started taking capoeira classes. I went to Mestre Marcelo's class because he was my sister's teacher and the only capoeira teacher I knew of at the time. Up to this point, my only athletic experiences were snowboarding and a year of track and field in high school. Capoeira's martial arts and gymnastic movements were totally new to me, and my body was unconditioned. My learning curve was steep. When I started capoeira, I couldn't hold a bridge position or do a cartwheel, and spinning kicks like *armada* were beyond me. But even though I felt awkward and sore most of the time, I enjoyed the learning process and kept coming back. After ten months, I participated in a batizado, a promotion ceremony, and received my first cordão.

Mestre Marcelo's classes gave me a good introduction to capoeira, but I never felt quite at home there. Mestre Marcelo was a good teacher, and I have a lot of respect for him, but something about the style of capoeira didn't appeal to me. Also, at age twenty, I was less than consistent and often distracted by events and circumstance. After about ten months I stopped taking capoeira classes. I wanted to continue with capoeira, I just didn't know where, how, or with whom.

# PART TWO

# Learn

CHAPTER SEVEN

# Capoeira 101

On a cold winter evening in Berkeley, I pulled up my motorcycle up in front of the address on the flyer. A sign read, "Baker's Martial Arts: Tai Kwan Do." A row of windows faced the street, but they were all fogged up. When I opened the door, I met with a blast of moist, warm air. Inside was a good sized dojo with red carpet and a big mural of a tiger on the wall.

A teacher stood and spoke to a class of about twenty-five men and women, all soaked in sweat. This was Mestre Acordeon. He was barrel-chested with a mostly salt beard, mostly pepper hair, and deep baritone voice. His Brazilian accent was so thick I couldn't understand much of what he said, but he spoke with great conviction and gestured expressively. When he went to an *atabaque* drum and whipped out a rat-a-tat triplet of notes, the students snapped to.

Mestre Acordeon commenced playing a steady rhythm, and the class moved in unison. Back and forth, step to step, all of them together. A crackle and pop from the drum, and all the students suddenly dropped close to the ground, spun into cartwheels, and kicked, all in time with the music. *Cool,* I thought.

Until I saw a flyer for this class, I had never heard of Mestre Acordeon. He had already published his book and established a reputation in capoeira circles, but he was a long way from the level of fame he would reach in later decades. When I went to Baker's Martial Arts that night, I had no idea what to expect. What I saw instantly interested me, and I began taking three classes a week.

Mestre Acordeon was intense and charismatic. He was often warm and humorous but not always gentle. Sometimes he yelled impatiently at his students for not understanding his intent. He demanded attention to detail, and stressed fundamentals. When he played capoeira with the students in the roda at the end of class, he moved with lightning speed and seemed always to know where his opponent was going to be next. He taught a grounded, pragmatic capoeira. The stance was low, the movements crisp and efficient, and there were not many superfluous elements. The games were intense, with an aggressive edge. The students were a diverse group who were serious about the training. They mostly ignored beginners like me, but I didn't mind. It seemed they were there to practice, learn, and train, not to socialize. I liked the no-nonsense style and intense rodas.

Soon I had full blown capoeira fever and spent all my spare time practicing or studying it. The more I learned, the more I wanted to learn. When I wasn't in class, I trained on my own in acrobatics, strength, endurance, and music. I read the few books in English about capoeira that existed back then, including Mestre Acordeon's *Capoeira: A Brazilian Art Form* and Nestor Capoeira's *The Little Capoeira Book,* both excellent resources to this day.

I read about how capoeira had evolved in Brazil from African roots over hundreds of years. During the colonial era, European traders shipped millions of enslaved people from western Africa to the Americas. Despite brutality and oppression, slaves in Brazil retained many of their African traditions, including stories, religion, dance, music, and martial arts. Some escaped captivity and fled into the jungle and mountainous wilderness. There, they formed *quilombos*— hidden villages of free African Brazilians.

The quilombos existed for decades, in some cases generations. The most famous is Quilombo dos Palmares, where the great leader Zumbi led a heroic but ill-fated resistance against colonial armies. Some researchers speculate that capoeira might have developed in these remote communities, but it is impossible to know. Much about the history of this art is unknown, as there is little documentation or evidence regarding it.

After Brazil abolished slavery in 1888, many newly free African Brazilians moved from rural plantations to urban centers along the coast and in the south. With no employment or opportunity for most of these people, social ills plagued the cities. During this period, capoeira became associated with illicit and criminal behavior. It was outlawed in 1890 and went underground. Fighters, thugs, bodyguards, and crooks practiced in secret. They adopted *apelidos*— nicknames—to make it harder for police to prosecute them. To this day, having an apelido is a capoeira tradition. The prohibition on capoeira lifted in 1920, but public prejudice remained for many years.

In 1937 a young master called Mestre Bimba (Manoel dos Reis Machado, 1899–1974) opened the first formal capoeira school in São Salvador, Bahia, Brazil. Mestre Bimba created a new style of capoeira, later called Capoeira *Regional*. He stripped much of the ritual and emphasized the combative aspects. His father had taught him the African fight game *batuque*, and Mestre Bimba brought in its sweeps and takedowns. He created a series of acrobatic throws, the *cintura desprezada*, to help students lose their fear of falling and land on their feet. Perhaps his most influential innovation was to develop the first systematic methodology for teaching capoeira. As part of this, he created a series of *seqüências*, sequences of movements done with a partner, that utilized the fundamental movements of capoeira. We still practice the *Seqüências de Mestre Bimba* today.

In addition to opening the first capoeira school, Mestre Bimba competed in bare-knuckled fighting matches. As he defeated fighters and representatives of various martial arts, capoeira's reputation grew. He and his students also performed publicly many times—including in 1953 for the president of Brazil, Getulio Vargas. Many of his students became teachers themselves, including Mestre Acordeon, who taught this new style of capoeira around Brazil and beyond. Despite all this, Mestre Bimba died impoverished and disillusioned with his lack of popular support. He would never know how much he had changed capoeira and helped it spread around the world.

From Mestre Acordeon's book and talking with him directly, I pieced together his career history. He had graduated from Mestre Bimba's school in 1959 and opened his first academy in 1962. In 1964 he and several friends founded the performance group Grupo Folclórico da Bahia, one of the first groups to present capoeira along with other African Brazilian art forms. These arts included *maculelê*, a folkloric martial art dance in which practitioners use two sticks or machetes in their hands, and *samba de roda*, a traditional form of *samba*, Brazil's national dance. The group toured Brazil for years and eventually internationally as well. Later I was fortunate to become friends with Mestre Gato, one of the founders of the famed capoeira group *Senzala*. He told me Acordeon's visit in 1966 had partly inspired and influenced the formation of this group.

In 1979, after a U.S. tour with his performance group Corpo Santo, Mestre Acordeon moved to California on a mission to transplant capoeira in a new land. The first time he taught capoeira in the U.S. was at Stanford University. This was capoeira's introduction to the West Coast and the second time it had been taught in the United States. Mestre Jelon had first taught capoeira in New York City in 1975. Mestre Acordeon has stayed in the U.S. ever since 1979, teaching, performing, and pioneering the spread of capoeira. By writing the first ever book about capoeira printed in English, recording almost a dozen albums of music, and teaching many thousands of students, he has raised capoeira's profile in North America and around the world as much as or more than anyone.

Fast forward to the early 1990s, and there I was, an Irish American kid falling in love with this African Brazilian art. It was so new and so foreign to us in the U.S, but that was part of its allure. There was so much to it, and it was unlike anything else. Already I was connected through Mestre Acordeon to Mestre Bimba and the roots of modern capoeira. Perhaps someday I could add something of value to the pioneering work of these giants. But for the moment I was just a speck, a nobody, trying to learn and absorb all the knowledge and skills of this rich cultural tradition.

My life in Berkeley revolved around my job and capoeira. I worked at the Bison on weekdays and weekend nights and trained capoeira weeknights and Saturday afternoons. On weeknights, capoeira class started at 8:00 p.m.. It was supposed to end at 10:00, but we usually stayed until 11:00, playing in long rodas or listening to Mestre Acordeon talk about strategy, music, history, or life in his native Bahia. I would often go home exhausted but too excited to sleep, thoughts of capoeira running through my head.

Most of the people in that group are long gone now, including most of the advanced students who came before me. The only ones from that generation still active today are Jordan and Suelly, who are mestres now. Although capoeira has developed significantly since then, these people amazed me with their speed, agility, and skill. I looked up to them and was inspired to be as good as them someday.

*At Ashkenaz, me on my head, Berkeley, California, c. 1993.*

Our capoeira was rough back then. Most of the people who were already practicing when I joined were more pugilistic than acrobatic. In class we practiced a lot of martial arts techniques, including takedowns, strikes, and throws. Capoeira is called a *jogo* (game), but in our rodas there were a lot of hard blows like *galopante* (open hand blow), *martelo*, (side kick), and takedowns. The more advanced students competed fiercely against each other and were not shy about roughing up us newbies now and again. I learned quickly to keep my guard up. If my kicks were high in the air, I risked an almost certain *rasteira*, (leg sweep).

I still remember the first time I got taken down hard. I did a straight kick and a senior student named Dianne, fast and precise, grabbed my leg and tossed me on my back. It was Brandon who gave me a broken rib, with a straight kick of his own. It was my fault for trying to do a *vingativa* takedown on him. Six weeks recovery taught me my lesson. I was mostly helpless until I had been training a couple of years. Then I started to get a few licks of my own in here and there.

Despite all this, we played with friendliness and a camaraderie that precluded anything from getting too serious. We learned to play hard from Mestre Acordeon, who played hard with us. But we were naive about how violent capoeira could get. In Brazil, capoeira was often much more intense and dangerous than the lighthearted rough-and-tumble of our North American practice. Some rodas devolved into little more than brawls, including vicious blows and unrestrained aggression.

About a year after I started training with Mestre Acordeon, a young mestre recently arrived from Brazil named Mestre Rã became our teacher as well. Mestre Rã and Mestre Acordeon had been friends for a few years, and in or around 1992 they decided to become business and teaching partners. This was the origin of the United Capoeira Association.

Shortly after Mestre Rã's arrival, a new wave of students started showing up to classes. First, Cravo and Canella, athletic youths who grew up around there. Years later Cravo and I would graduate together. Soon after them came Recruta, Papagaio, Pimenta, Espanta Leão, Carrapicho, Fogueira, Marreta, and others. These young men and women were highly talented, and fast learners. They quickly developed amazing skills beyond anything I could do. I admired them, but it was discouraging too. I was so slow to learn. Was it even worth it, to be putting all this time and energy into capoeira?

I reconsidered my involvement in the art, and asked myself what I hoped to accomplish with capoeira. For one, I wanted to train hard until I was good at capoeira. Actually, better than "good," I wanted to be "great," whatever that means. For me it meant being able to do explosive acrobatic movements, know all the music, and be able to hold my own with the best. That I didn't have half the talent of many other students was a setback. But I had persistence and dogged determination. I could work out like a fiend, study hard, and get lots of experience. I made a bet that these could make up for lack of talent.

In order to get good at capoeira, I had to keep practicing it for the long run. How could I make it a big enough part of my life that it would have roots? For most people, because of demands in their lives, capoeira remained a hobby, or is eventually given up altogether. For me it had to be a lifestyle.

A vague idea had been tumbling around in the back of my mind ever since Royal Gorge. It was about capoeira, and my future. Suddenly it became clear: I could be a capoeira teacher. That was it! I could graduate and open my own capoeira school. That would be my job. Not only would this cement capoeira's place in my life, but it would allow me to keep training hard for as long as it took. And, even more importantly, this could be a way to realize my life goals: to live an extraordinary life, have a unique career, and make a positive impact.

To my knowledge a North American had never graduated and opened their own actual capoeira studio. I might be the first. Even if I wasn't, these were essentially uncharted waters, ones that I could explore and craft my own unique path through. And, if I could pass to future generations all the things capoeira gave me, including culture, community, fitness, and excitement, then that would be making the world a better place. Plus, a successful career with capoeira would allow me to remain independent, free of the corporate interests I loathed.

It would take several years to flesh out the plan, but from that day on I knew my career was going to be teaching capoeira. Relieved and excited to finally figure out my direction, I threw myself into the training with renewed passion. From then on I made learning capoeira my focus and priority. Whatever else I did was scheduled around it; whatever decisions I made were based on my career goals. I also stopped worrying so much about other students more talented than me. I just worried about my own path and progress, and then began to enjoy the process more.

One night in class, we had visitors from Brazil. Two young men from Capoeira Regional group called Abada, they had powerful builds, serious expressions, and immaculate movements. Mestre Acordeon gave a short class, and then we gathered for the roda.

After one relatively slow, relaxed game between two of our students, I stepped up to the *pé do berimbau*: the foot of the berimbau. This is where each game starts. I was opposite Max, one of the Brazilian visitors. I shook his hand and smiled at him, but he didn't return the expression.

I had been training for three or four years and knew enough to play a simple game, avoid some of the most obvious traps and attacks, and engage opponents on an intermediate level. I was not experienced enough to compete on a high level, as I had learned, so I approached this game with caution. First I did an *aú* into the roda and began to step side to side in the *ginga*, capoeira's basic step. Max kept his distance, executing a few kicks high and nowhere near me. It seemed he was playing nice and respectfully. I appreciated this, as I had no appetite for trading blows with this guy. So when I did a martelo toward Max's head, and he didn't dodge or block it, I thought I was doing the right thing by stopping it short of his face by a few inches and retracting it quickly.

Apparently Max took my martelo another way, perhaps incensed I would even consider kicking toward his head. Next thing I knew, he suddenly rushed at me. Quickly dropping below my center of gravity, he reached one arm between my legs and the other over my shoulder. Lifting me over his head as if I were little more than a rag doll, he then thew me out of the roda and against a nearby wall. I was stunned, and helpless to defend myself.

As I picked myself up off the ground, the music stopped. I think everyone was kind of shocked. Then Mestre Rã was stepping between me and Max, who was still coming after me. Mestre Rã calmed him down, and the roda resumed. The mood was subdued now, and I just watched.

The bruises I suffered that night were minor, but I felt humiliated. That guy had totally manhandled me. If it wasn't for my mestre, he probably would have beat the crap out of me. Once again I had been taught a lesson. Capoeira was more dangerous than I had known. I threw myself into training with a new urgency, vowing to prevent this from ever happening again.

# CHAPTER EIGHT

# A Portrait of Two Mestres

O ur capoeira group went through a downturn, and sometimes I was the only student in class with one of the mestres. From this one-on-one time I progressed faster, plus gained insight into my teachers' individual personalities and philosophies.

The two mestres contrasted starkly. Mestre Acordeon was gruff and intense, an old-school martial arts master who demanded serious commitment and hard work. He rarely gave compliments and always wanted more and better results. Mestre Rã would yell and curse in Portuguese at us to energize the group, but on an individual basis was easygoing and patient. He was youthful and athletic, while Mestre Acordeon was older and crafty. Mestre Acordeon stressed fundamentals and martial arts and had us do countless repetitions of basic movements and takedowns. Mestre Rã showed us fancy acrobatics, complicated sequences, and advanced techniques.

Each teacher had tremendous strengths, and as a team they presented a powerful and complete instructional package. I loved training with both of them, relating to their contrasting approaches and personalities in different ways.

Mestre Rã was part elite athlete, part Zen master, and part *malandro*. The malandro is an archetypical character in capoeira culture, a devil-may-care rascal who lives by his own rules and wits. The malandro cannot be bothered with a nine-to-five job, preferring to survive through hustle and craftiness. Historically, the malandro was found on street corners, in bars, gambling, playing capoeira, chasing women, or leisurely sleeping in. This is not to say Mestre Rã was like this—he worked hard to succeed in the U.S. But he always had a rogue edge.

Mestre Rã was fierce in his teaching and playing of capoeira. He would often yell at us, cursing us in Portuguese, demanding we increase intensity or speed. It wasn't anger—it was passion. Every game was a battle. A joyful battle, but a battle to the end, which he usually celebrated with a hug. In conversation, on the other hand, Mestre Rã was relaxed, exuding an air of non attachment. Little perturbed him, and I almost never saw him angry. He easily let people, possessions, and situations come and go from his life. Rarely did he talk about the past, and never with nostalgia. In class, between yelling at us and tossing us around in the roda, he lightly offered individual suggestions and instruction. When students showed good attention and made improvements he offered praise and encouragement, but if a student failed to make progress he seemed unperturbed.

Mestre Rã's capoeira movements and game were amazing to watch, combining a dancer's grace and a boxer's pugnacity. His acrobatics were impressive. One minute he'd be flying in his signature *folha seca*, (a windmill flip), and the next *rolé* spin into a *macaco* (type of back handspring). His ginga was grounded, dynamic, and expressive, and his kicks dangerously powerful. He loved to play rough, including medium-to-hard contact with kicks and full-throttle takedowns. He traded blows and sweeps without a shadow of rancor, insisting this kind of contact was a favor, never done from anger or desire to harm.

*Mestre Rã and Mestre Acordeon, Berkeley, c. 1993.*

This is not to say he was kicking or being kicked all the time. He had a finely tuned sense of strategy and delighted in the dialogue of capoeira games. He told us many times, "Let the game cook," meaning we must allow time for these aspects to develop. Mestre Rã's training habits were as inspiring as his game. He was always in the gym working on strength and conditioning and ate a strict diet augmented by the latest supplements. In class he led most drills by example, completing them along with the students.

Mestre Acordeon was more of an enigma. The more I learned about him, the more I realized I didn't know much about him or capoeira. To take a class with him was to chase him on a journey, striving to keep up mentally and straining your body's limits. He emphasized fundamentals, but at the same time each class was creative and unique. The workouts were phenomenal, but understanding Mestre Acordeon's thought process and philosophy was the deeper lesson, one that took years to learn.

In the roda, Mestre Acordeon was a dominating force, outmaneuvering most opponents easily. The only people I ever saw gain any kind of advantage over him were other top level mestres. He was in his late forties and had lost some of his acrobatic skills—I heard he was the first to do a back flip in the roda. Nevertheless, he was lightning quick, changing direction or reacting to an opponent in the blink of an eye. But what made him so difficult to oppose—still to this day—were his perception and instinct. Like a master chess player, he always saw several moves ahead. If you tried to move to a spot, he was already there. When you launched a kick, he was always in position to sweep or trip you. He liked to play rough, and I along with many others received his bruising kicks and hard takedowns. He and Mestre Rã had many roda battles, which occasionally resulted in wrestling matches, neither one willing to give quarter to the other.

Mestre Acordeon lived like he played capoeira—dynamically, always moving and creating. Throughout his life, he expressed capoeira's characteristic creativity, adaptability, and unpredictability. Like a good capoeirista playing the jogo, he traveled in a continuous series of creative movements, seldom repeating the same pattern. He was an adventurer and pioneer, constantly exploring new areas both geographical and artistic. He was rarely content to sit still and enjoy the fruits of his labor, preferring instead to move into a new endeavor. His creative process was free flowing and ever evolving. His plans lasted only as long as they helped him realize his objective and often changed along the way. He was ever pursuing a new venture, creative goal, and expansion of his experience and capabilities. Because he was constantly changing, he was difficult to predict or understand. He is a true capoeirista in every aspect of life.

His teaching style emphasized the basics—the *arroz e feijão*, or rice and beans, as he would say. But he also created new sequences, explored new applications, and wrote new songs. And in his creative process all of our envelopes were pushed. No two classes were ever the same. He drove us both physically and mentally to transcend our perceived limitations.

Mestre Acordeon instructed us extensively in playing the traditional music of capoeira, including the rhythms of the berimbau, as well as related arts maculelê, samba de roda, *afoxé, samba reggae,* and *puxada de rede.* We were expected to learn it all, and to be able to sing songs in Portuguese too. In addition to the traditional arrangements, he regularly created new compositions, challenging us to keep up.

At the end of class, after the roda, Mestre Acordeon usually gave a talk long past the intended hour. His speeches wandered from topic to topic, but always shared a trove of valuable information. After commenting on strategy and the jogos we had just played, he spoke of history, philosophy, his childhood in Bahia, and the lessons he learned from Mestre Bimba. Explaining in detail capoeira's culture and ritual, he strove to give his North American audience an understanding of this foreign art's subtleties.

Sometimes Mestre Acordeon's fluidity challenged people's flexibility. For example, we might have carefully crafted a plan for a performance or public demonstration. Five minutes before it started, he would announce an entirely new plan, and we were all expected to adapt. In class, his instructions were often difficult to understand or seemingly contradictory. Some students showed frustration with this, and I myself struggled at times to remain appreciative. Eventually, though, I came to see this unpredictability as part of our capoeira training. The challenge wasn't just to perform a sequence of physical moves, but also to follow a sequence of mental shifts. Learning a great master's creative process was the lesson. After many years, I began to predict where he was going. At that point I was put at the front of the class, because the front row consists of the students who best understand the master's wishes.

Despite, or perhaps because of, Mestre Acordeon's capriciousness, he is undeniably a creative genius. His body of work is enormous and includes teaching, performing, writing, recording music, and pioneering capoeira. Like his master before him, he is an innovator who has substantially influenced the capoeira world. His extensive international teaching and published work have helped capoeira evolve. It is not an overstatement to say Mestre Acordeon has helped to shape modern capoeira.

Back in the 1990s, most of us studying with Mestre Acordeon didn't grasp the extent of his stature. He had not yet cemented his legacy, although he had already accomplished a lot. Capoeira was small in the U.S., and we didn't know about his already considerable reputation and influence in Brazil and around the globe. We saw him as a great capoeirista, inspiring teacher, and powerful personality, but we did not realize he was a living legend, destined to be an internationally recognized artist and authority. As much as I valued my many years and countless hours training directly with him, it was only later that I came to appreciate what a great privilege this was.

It was fascinating and revealing to watch the relationship between these two mestres, with their strong personalities. The influence of each moderated the other's extremes. Mestre Acordeon was dominant and controlling. Though Mestre Rã was laid-back and relaxed, he still had strong opinions and would not always give way. Overt conflict never surfaced in public, but it was clear the two occasionally clashed. During one period, after a couple years of working together, they seemed to experience a rough patch in the relationship. But they held it together and worked it out, and we students benefited.

At different points, both mestres physically tested my willingness to stand up for myself. First it was Mestre Rã. He played hard with everyone, and I think all of us received a blow or takedown from him at least a couple of times. During one period, he was particularly hard on me. I had developed a decent game and some skills—not expertise, but enough to make me one of the more advanced students in class. When I played Mestre Rã, he became even more aggressive than usual. I didn't mind too much because even though he was far out of my league, I liked playing rough and enjoyed the challenge.

One night in the roda, it came to a head. Mestre Rã and I shook hands and cartwheeled in to start our game. Almost immediately, he launched a martelo kick to my head. It was too fast and well-timed for me to dodge or block it, and it hit my temple. For a second my vision blacked out, and I saw stars. I felt disorientated, but I continued to ginga, trying not to be an easy target while I regained my senses. A moment later he came at me with the same kick, hitting my head again with the same result. I was in trouble. This was not a game anymore—closer to a fight. Mestre Rã was fast, strong, and skillful. I had to find a way to protect myself. I had a feeling he would try a martelo a third time. I would try to take him down when he did.

Sure enough, Mestre Rã launched another martelo. As his foot shot up, I rushed in at him. I grabbed under his kicking leg and secured it with my arm, stepping in to do a *banda*, a lift and sweep takedown, as my mestres had taught me. My positioning and technique were poor, and I could not sweep him cleanly to the ground. I wasn't willing to give up the advantage, though, so I held on to his leg and charged forward hard. Driving him backward outside of the roda and to the ground, I went down with him. As he crashed to the floor, I fell on top of him and intentionally smashed my forearm into his face. I hit his mouth, and immediately blood came from his lip.

As the other students looked on dumbstruck, Mestre Acordeon jumped up and separated us. "What are you doing, man? Calm down!"

I felt indignant. "I had to do something! He was kicking my ass!"

Mestre Rã seemed calm, unbothered by the interaction. He rose to his feet and told us both there was no problem. Wiping the blood from his lip, he invited me back into the roda. I joined him cautiously. We shook hands and played for a few more moments, keeping our distance and with no contact. After that, Mestre Rã never kicked me like that again. We played hard at times, but to a limit. From then on, he always showed me respect both in the roda and out. He was testing me that night, not so much my physical skills but to see if I would stick up for myself. If I had failed to do so, I would have failed the test.

About a year later, a similar episode happened with Mestre Acordeon. Again, I did not mind getting roughed up a bit in the roda. I considered it part of good martial arts training. Now, though, it was increasing, and with Mestre Acordeon it was both in the roda and during training.

A pattern was developing, and I decided to speak to him about it. I didn't want to do it in front of other students, though, and he and I seldom talked on the phone or met outside of class back in those days. An opportunity presented itself one Saturday at a class at Ashkenaz, the venerable Berkeley music hall and community center.

The only people there were Suelly, Mestre Acordeon, and me. Mestre Acordeon had Suelly and I work some partner drills, attack and defense exchanges. As we repeated the sequences over and over, he gave instructions and feedback. He kept telling me to keep my arms up, to guard my face. Apparently I wasn't doing so to his satisfaction, so he cut in and began the drill with me. As I completed a kick, I let my guard down, and he slapped me hard on the side of my head with a galopante.

I reeled back, my ear ringing. I realized this was the moment I had been waiting for. I stepped back and held up my open hands to signal a timeout. I was angry but kept my voice even. "Mestre."

"Yes?" He was nonchalant.

"Look, Mestre. I come here to learn capoeira, not for you to beat me up." I looked him in the eye.

"Oooooo," said Suelly. It was not often someone openly stood up to Mestre Acordeon.

Mestre Acordeon stood still for a moment, looking at me. He seemed to be measuring me and the situation. Finally he laughed deeply, dispelling the tension and signaling truce. Clapping my shoulder he said, "Okay, Galego. I understand. You got it."

From then on Mestre Acordeon stopped roughing me up. He also showed me more respect in general. In the roda he continued to play me hard, but he pulled back the harder blows. Outside the game, he seemed to give weight to my positions in a new way.

Both teachers had tested me to see if I would stand up for myself, if I would insist on their respect. They hadn't wanted me to retreat, roll over, or submit. They wanted me to fight back, to defend myself. I passed the test because I had done what it took, however inelegant, to hold my ground with each of them. But they also passed a test with me. I didn't mind them testing my boundaries, seeing if I'd stand up for myself. Rather, I appreciated the opportunity to discover my own strength. And it showed me they had the strength and conviction to challenge me on all fronts to do better.

I had participated in a fair amount of capoeira in the U.S. and Brazil by this point and felt confident that Mestre Acordeon and Mestre Rã were top-of-the-line teachers. Each of them was a true master of a rich and complex art form. I believe they were two of the most skilled and knowledgeable capoeira teachers anywhere. Beyond being instructors, they were artists, dancers, fighters, athletes, and leaders.

As the years passed, I slowly grasped the depth of knowledge these mestres were passing on to us. There were so many topics to cover. Martial arts, including blows, defense, throws, and strategy. Acrobatics with countless variations. The music alone could be its own course of study, including various instruments, the many capoeira rhythms, and both traditional and modern songs. Philosophy, etiquette, customs, traditions, Portuguese language, and ritual. On top of all this were related art forms including maculelê and samba de roda, which were also part of our curriculum.

For teachers to pass on all of this information to students takes years of sustained, consistent training. We might train a sequence using the *chapa giratório,* spinning side kick, for a week, and then not revisit that technique for a year or two. This was true for all but the most core components. Each week, in addition to practicing the fundamentals, we would explore particular advanced techniques and related topics. Over the course of years, a tapestry of knowledge was woven. Anything less than many years with these two great mestres would give only a partial picture of the traditions they were passing on.

Learning techniques was important, but there was more to the learning process than absorbing the curriculum. I trained with Mestre Acordeon and Mestre Rã for ten years, and I gained not just an understanding of the techniques, but of the mestres themselves. By the time I graduated, I had a deep sense of their philosophies and embodiments of capoeira. This was essential in carrying on the lineage. One day I would be on my own, teaching my own students. When that day came, I would need to rely on my understanding of my mestres and their visions in order to further their legacy.

# CHAPTER NINE

# Water to Drink

Capoeira is a traditional art with roots going back 500 years or more. It has evolved throughout its history, adapting to societal pressure, cultural change, and passing generations. In the 1990s its evolution continued, now not only in Brazil but around the world. Our group and others grew and developed, becoming part of the spread and history of capoeira. In the U.S., students' skills reached ever higher levels, and new teachers and groups appeared often. I heard there was capoeira in places like Europe and Japan now too.

Brazil had many thousands of capoeira schools with many different styles. In some, the Capoeira Regional trend progressed to an extreme, little resembling Mestre Bimba's work. The focus on athletic and effective martial arts had resulted in high levels of physical skill. But unfortunately, violence and aggression were also common. Sometimes rodas devolved into fights, which still happens to this day. It's usually bullies, using brute force to hog the roda. Fortunately, now it is less frequent than it was back then, and more capoeira teachers promote inclusiveness and respect.

A few teachers stayed true to Mestre Bimba's original Capoeira Regional, including Mestre Acordeon and Mestre Bimba's son Mestre Nenel. These schools have preserved the tradition, even while exploring new skills and variations. Meanwhile, other movements have taken capoeira in new directions, like the *Miudinho* style for example, which recalls some of the playful, lighthearted capoeira of an earlier age, while taking the athleticism of modern capoeira to an even higher level.

Another contrasting movement to Regional is the Capoeira *Angola* style. This form is more ritualistic and theatrical and emphasizes the strategy of *malicia*—trickiness and deception. Angola comes from old-school Bahia, largely from Mestre Pastinha, a contemporary of Mestre Bimba. Mestre Pastinha opened a Capoeira Angola school in 1941 in Bahia, and many of today's Angola mestres are his students. Prominent Capoeira Angola mestres from other lineages include Mestre Nô and my friend Mestre Boa Gente.

At that time, there were only a handful of capoeira teachers in the U.S., mostly on the East and West Coasts, and no teachers had their own academies. Classes happened at dance studios, martial arts schools, and community centers. Mestre Acordeon briefly had a space in Oakland but gave it up. His group in the Bay Area and Mestre Jelon's in New York were the oldest and most established, but even these had only a few dozen students each. For the most part, capoeira groups were isolated pockets of activity. Batizados or other occasions for different groups to mix with each other were rare.

In early 1993, a group of Mestre Acordeon's students went with him to the town of Ukiah. It was a rural community about two hours' drive north of the Bay Area and home to a surprisingly robust capoeira scene. One of Mestre Acordeon's first graduated students, Amunka, had teamed up with a Brazilian mestre named Rony. The two made a dynamic and charismatic pair, similar to Mestre Acordeon and Mestre Rã in some ways, and had attracted a lot of students. Amunka was a kind, gentle man originally from Guatemala. He approached capoeira with a playful, enlightened perspective. Mestre Rony was a gregarious jokester with a dynamic game, including amazing back-handsprings. Their students were an eclectic group of dancers, martial artists, aging hippies, and athletic teenagers.

The teachers put on a weekend of workshops and held a batizado where they graduated a large group of their students. It was here I first met Mestre Amen, who had pioneered capoeira in Los Angeles and appeared in the film *Only the Strong*.

*One of many jogos between Cravo and I, Berkeley, c. 1995.*

*Only the Strong* is the only Hollywood production to date with capoeira central in its theme. The main character teaches capoeira to troubled inner-city youths and uses it to defeat bad guys. It's a martial arts action movie. Though it simplifies capoeira and liberally employs clichés, it is fun and unpretentious. Its release marked the first appearance of capoeira in U.S. mass media and was instrumental in introducing it to the public. When it first arrived at a theatre in Emeryville, California, our group did a demonstration out front. Twenty-five years later, I would still meet new students who said they discovered capoeira through *Only the Strong*.

Playing capoeira with students and teachers from different schools helped test and develop my skills. The fundamentals Mestre Acordeon and Mestre Rã taught served me well, but it took a while to learn how to apply them and cope with different strategies and forms. The first times I played *Angoleiros*, I was especially thrown off. Superfluous gestures confused and distracted me. I bit on fakes and feints. A couple times I got kicked or swept. Eventually I learned to ignore the theatrics and subterfuge and concentrate on my opponent's center of gravity, keeping up with the important movements and dictating with my own.

It was around this time a talented young Brazilian capoeirista named Calango started hanging around with our group. Calango was amazingly acrobatic and already a master martial artist. He always played capoeira with joy and was never bulling or aggressive. He was a great example of what to aspire to. I never did half of his moves, but my games with him back then were some of the best games I ever played.

I took capoeira classes three or four times a week and practiced music and movements on my own most other days. For cross training, I ran, biked, weight trained, and played basketball. In my mid-twenties and having practiced capoeira steadily for five years, I was in the best shape of my life. I was finally learning advanced acrobatic movements like macaco, *volta por cima* (a low back walkover), and *parafuso* (a jumping spin kick). But then there was the back flip.

A back flip, as in to jump up and backward, do a full rotation in the air, and land on your feet, was the crown jewel of acrobatics. It was a threshold everyone wanted to pass. If you could do a back flip, you were legitimate. All the really exciting and skilled capoeiristas could do a back flip.

Learning to flip was difficult for me. Early attempts resulted in my landing on my head. So I began taking gymnastic lessons at a local gym called Head Over Heels. This athletic playground, full of trampolines, foam pits, spring floors, trapezes, ropes, bars, beams, and all manner of training gear, was like paradise for me. I ended up getting a job there coaching kids classes, which taught me a lot about teaching.

Through quality coaching, lots of training, and soft foam pads, I finally learned to do a flip. On the padded floor at least, I could do a standing back tuck and a roundoff back tuck. Of course, it took a lot more practice to do flips in a roda or performance. It finally all came together one time when our capoeira group did a big presentation in the "How Berkeley Can You Be?" parade. Mestre Acordeon and Mestre Rã led the *batucada* percussion line up a crowded University Avenue, and several of us students took turns doing acrobatics in front. After years of working at it, I was confident and my skills were strong. That day I did twelve roundoff-back flips in the parade.

On the path of learning capoeira I found myself on another journey as well, an internal one. It was process of understanding my own emotions, and of self-mastery. Mestre Acordeon says that the roda is a metaphor for life, that in it, you encounter the same emotions we experience in our lives. In capoeira there is joy, excitement, happiness, anger, fear, love, and even hate. Part of capoeira's lesson is to not be controlled by our emotions, especially the negative ones like anger and fear. We learn to feel them but not lose control to them.

Sometime in the late '90s I attended a batizado held by Mestre Marcelo. It was a large event with many capoeiristas from all over the U.S. and Brazil. For some reason I arrived late. The ceremony in which students earned new cords was ending, and the roda was opening for anybody to play. I maneuvered to a position near the *orquestra*, the orchestra, to enter the roda. In the crowd across the circle from me, who did I see? Max, my old nemesis who had thrown me out of the roda at Baker's Martial Arts years before. I felt an adrenaline rush at the sight of him. Ignoring the butterflies in my stomach, I went to the pé do berimbau and squatted down to play.

Max broke from the crowd and squatted down at the pé do berimbau too, deliberately taking position to play me. I had thought he wouldn't remember me, but it seemed he did. I certainly remembered him, and was pretty sure how this game was going to go. Hairs rose on the back of my neck. I thought, *I can't let this dude get me again*. Anger and fear welled up inside me. I took a deep breath and forced myself to calm down. Approaching Max, I extended my hand, but this time I didn't bother to smile.

After a brief handshake, I did a quick rolê spin into the roda. This move protects you from a hard head-butt or other blow that could knock you on your back during a cartwheel. I went into my ginga, keeping my stance low and my guard up. After a few cursory kicks, spins, and feints, I sensed things were coming to a head. Sure enough, without waiting for any perceived provocation, Max lunged at me. He came in low, attempting to get under my center of gravity and grab me as he had before. This time I was prepared. I sprawled my legs out behind me to escape his grasp, the way my mestres had taught me. Pushing down on his back with one arm, I threaded the other under his chin and against his neck. With his head under my arm, I tightened my chokehold. He continued to drive forward and tried to grab my legs while I worked my arm ever tighter under his windpipe to cut off his air supply.

We continued in this struggle for several seconds, and then the mestres crowded around us, breaking us apart. Unwilling to give up my position until he gave up his, I continued to choke him for a few more seconds until I felt him stop going for my legs. Then I loosened my hold on his neck and let the mestres drag us apart.

After Max and I were separated, Mestre Marcelo insisted we shake hands. We did, briefly and without eye contact. I knew it had been ugly, but I didn't care. At least I had kept my composure, used my training, and defended myself from being thrown around again. Perhaps it had been no more than a stalemate, but I was okay with that.

In his book *Capoeira: A Brazilian Art Form*, Mestre Acordeon describes stages of a capoeirista's development. In the first stage, called "playing in the dark," capoeiristas have learned many movements but have little understanding of the jogo. When they jump into the roda, they don't understand what is happening, not perceiving the dialogue of movement that is capoeira. As if in the dark, they can't see the movements of their opponents, whose attacks seem to materialize out of thin air.

Eventually experience and training bump the capoeirista to a new plateau. Suddenly, as if a light were turned on, they can see their opponents' movements as they occur and keep up with them. Now they can engage their adversaries in an improvised dialogue, rather than just move on their own or react too late.

There was one particular jogo when the lights switched on for me. It was just another roda at Baker's. As I shook hands with my opponent, I was kind of spaced out, absentmindedly listening to the music. Mestre Rã was singing a song: "Manda um abraço pra ela, Capoeira me chamou...," meaning "Send her a hug, capoeira called me..."

As I cartwheeled into the circle, I had a strange feeling, almost like I was removed from my body and watching it move. Then I found myself effortlessly dodging, kicking, and *playing* with other person. It seemed like I could predict their movements and positions. At the same time, I was hearing the music and every move I made was locked into the rhythm. Duck a kick on a downbeat, deliver the counterattack on the next, spin on my head as the berimbau calls.

Up until this time I had been mostly bouncing around on my own in the roda. I might or might not have done some good movements, but they had little to do with my opponent, much less the music. This was how anyone begins, just acting out a pantomime of the game, and "playing in the dark." But now something had clicked, illumination had occurred. Only just now was I "playing in the light," and it was thrilling.

There's a phrase you hear not only in capoeira songs, but also in Brazilian popular music including the famous bossa nova standard by Antonio Carlos Jobim. "*Água de beber*" means "water to drink," and Mestre Acordeon describes it in his book as another metaphor, one that means a source of understanding, or quenching the thirst for knowledge and experience.

I took it to mean even more. I thought of "Água de beber" as an answer to a riddle, an oasis in the desert, or a quest completed. Learning a back flip, "playing in the light," and mastering my emotions were the completion of important steps on my capoeira path. They were "water to drink" on my thirsty journey to becoming a capoeira teacher.

# CHAPTER TEN

# On the Road

L eaving my hostel on foot, I emerged onto O'Connell Street, a wide boulevard adorned with the statues of Irish republican heroes. Across the street was the General Post Office with its huge neoclassical pillars. It was here that the 1916 uprising began, when Patrick Pearse and James Connolly with their band of rebels seized the building and declared it the headquarters of a free Ireland. Bullet holes from the ensuing British siege still riddled the exterior wall, left there as a testament to their courage.

Crossing the River Liffey, I entered the Temple Bar district with its cobbled streets. Cozy-looking pubs called to me. *Later,* I thought. After passing Dublin Castle's hulk and zigzagging to St. Stephen's Green Park, I rested for a while in the shade of lush trees. Leaving the oasis of green and calm, I walked up Grafton Street. This pedestrian-only area bustled with shoppers, tourists, and artists. A juggler entertained a small crowd on one corner, and a little farther down a fiddler played lively tunes while money slowly accumulated in his violin case.

Finally I reached my destination: Trinity College, home to the ancient *Book of Kells*. This treasure of literature and art dates back to 800 CE, and I was excited to see this link to my Celtic heritage with my own eyes. Passing between stone spires and under buttressed arches, I made my way to the museum. Twenty-two Irish pounds for entry. *What? I can't afford that!* Once again, I was traveling on a shoestring, having saved up enough money from restaurant work for a roundtrip ticket from California to Ireland. I had about $20 a day for food, lodging, and transportation. Disappointed, I walked back across town to my hostel.

I was solo backpacking through the Republic of Ireland on a three-week trip. I had always wanted to visit the land of my ancestors—my father's people came from County Cork, and my mother's from County Sligo. As a child I read Irish myths and legends, and later W. B. Yeats's poetry and James Joyce's prose gave me a picture of Irish life. And ever since that Waterboys tape in Egypt, Celtic music had captivated me. Embarking on a now familiar routine, I had saved a little money, packed a bag, and caught a flight.

In Dublin, I spent two more days exploring its streets before taking a bus headed south. A couple days' travel through green rolling hills of pasture and forest brought me to County Wicklow, then on to Waterford, the source of famous crystal. Next, I made my way to County Kerry on the West Coast. Kerry had a raw, stark beauty but also seemed empty and impoverished. Here in this out-of-the-way corner of Ireland was the legacy of hundreds of years of subjugation to English rule and persistent economic depression. Many of the country homes were little more than mud huts with thatched roofs. The surrounding countryside was mostly barren fields, crisscrossed by crumbling stone walls. The people were kindly enough, but seemed somehow myopic, as if the outside world had forgotten them, and they had in turn forgotten it. The place felt lonely, disjoined from the rest of Europe, and I continued north toward Galway.

As my bus came over a rise, I caught my first sight of Galway City. Nestled along a sheltered bay, a collection of colorful and stately structures crowded the shoreline and extended in tendrils into the surrounding countryside. Spired churches, elegant civic buildings, and quaint homes and businesses stood side by side. A large central park was lush and green. Rays of sunlight reflected off the waves of Galway Bay, which stretched into the Atlantic Ocean. In the distance the Aran Islands, the last land this side of the Americas, guarded the entrance to the bay. Galway is the westernmost city of all of Europe, once considered to be at the end of the world.

The town's old-world charm and beautiful surrounding countryside harkened back to an earlier time. Western Ireland is the cradle of Celtic culture, and nowhere more so than Galway. From open pub doors I heard wisps of fiddle music and occasionally heard the Gaelic language spoken. Open-doored artist studios displayed paintings and sculptures. The mood and culture of the place were different from anywhere else I had been. It was calm, traditional, and simple, yet it also hummed with creativity and life. Perched out here on the continent's westernmost point, pressed constantly by the forces of nature, the community beamed like a Celtic lighthouse.

One night a handful of backpackers at my hostel invited me to a pub for live traditional music. Entering the establishment, we took in a lively scene. Many dozens of people had crowded into the compact space, mostly locals by the look of them. Men and women crowded the bar, calling for pints and conversing noisily. A ring of musicians played a lively tune on a variety of instruments. There were several fiddles, a couple of guitars, some whistles, a kind of bagpipe, a banjo, and one bodhrán drum. The musicians appeared to be in a trance, their faces expressionless. Their fingers, though, performed a sprightly dance on their instruments, and the music was pure life. Melodies lilted and careened, tempo surged and receded. Jigs, reels, waltzes, and airs, tumbled out one after the next.

I was transfixed. As my acquaintances moved to the bar, I stopped and devoted my attention to the musicians. The music was mesmerizing and beautiful, and it called to something deep inside me. Each melody suggested a story of heroic glory, joyful romp, or tragic romance, a tapestry of sound that echoed an ancient age. I sat and listened all night, and it was a pleasure to do so, but I thought about what a joy it must be to actually play music like this. *Someday.*

The next day I set out on my own to explore the surrounding country by bus. I headed toward Connemara, the rugged, lonely land that juts into the ocean at Ireland's northwest corner. This area is known as the *Gaeltacht*, where Irish Gaelic is still the dominant language in the few inhabited areas. As we passed the village of Spiddal, gray-green mountains loomed to the right. On the left, shimmering Galway Bay opened into the Atlantic. The road narrowed, and there was less evidence of people. Soon we were passing through a wild expanse, a primordial domain of rock, bog, forest, and water. Even within the rumbling bus, a deep sense of quiet permeated. The wilderness's calm was punctuated only by a gale of wind, the pitter-patter of a momentary bout of rain, the lonesome call of a bird, and the rumbling of our out-of-place, manmade contraption.

As the bus continued west to Ireland's far reaches, riders exited one by one at tiny villages or empty crossroads, until I was the only passenger left. Staring out at the beautiful, barren landscape, I was spellbound. Occasionally a ray of sunlight broke through the rolling clouds, illuminating a patch of land in a blazing pool of brilliance. Boulder-strewn valleys with rich green heather breached the mountain heights, mist shrouding their mysterious reaches. It felt like an ancient land, one that had little changed in a thousand years. I remembered the mighty heroes I had read about as a child, those who had wandered and fought on these lands. My ancestors could have passed this way ages before.

The bus left the coast and headed north into the rocky hills. In a wide valley, we passed a solitary lake with deep black waters and a small forested island in the middle. The rugged and lonely place felt weirdly familiar to me, and I had a strong sense of deja vu. Maybe it was because it reminded me of the beginning of my favorite poem, Yeats's "The Stolen Child":

> *Where dips the rocky highland*
> *Of Sleuth Wood in the lake,*
> *There lies a leafy island*
> *Where flapping herons wake*
> *The drowsy water rats;*
> *There we've hid our faery vats,*
> *Full of berries*
> *And of reddest stolen cherries.*
> *Come away, O human child!*
> *To the waters and the wild*
> *With a faery, hand in hand,*
> *For the world's more full of weeping*
> *than you can understand.*

The next day I left Galway to head north to County Sligo, home of my mother's side of the family. From there I set out on foot to Ballisodare village, where my mother's ancestors had lived. She had given me the phone number of living relatives here whom she had tracked down when visiting Ireland years before. I walked the several miles to the village, passing through suburbs, then green countryside. It was another sunny day, and I had a great view of Ben Bulben Mountain looming behind Sligo town. In the Irish folk tales I had read as a child, this hill was part of the famous hero Finn

McCool's hunting grounds, and the center of the great warrior-queen Maeve's realm.

I came upon the community cemetery in the center of Ballisodare. Wandering between gravestones ancient and new, I scanned them for any ancestors of mine. My mother's family was called Gray, and I inherited my middle name from her grandfather Louis Gray. He had come to the U.S. by boat in 1917, leaving behind family and a sweetheart he would never see again.

There they were! Lined up in a back row of the cemetery were six gravestones with the name Gray. The oldest of them dated from the 1800s, meaning they were probably Louis Gray's parents, or grandparents. That made them my great-great-grandparents. I felt like I had accomplished a mission. I had come to see the land of my ancestors, and this was literally it. I thought about my family history and what the lives of these people might have been like. Realistically there was a good chance their lives were sad, full of poverty and tragedy. They had been Catholics in Ireland, suffering the great Potato Famine and brutal English rule.

I crossed the road and was almost run over by a car. I still wasn't used to traffic going in the opposite direction than in the U.S. and had looked in the wrong direction. How ironic it would have been to perish at this spot, a few feet from my ancestors' graves, thus completing a morbid circle.

A phone booth stood by the road. Dialing the number my mother had given me, I asked for the Grays, and a young man politely asked who I was. I clumsily explained I was an American relative, currently in Ballisodare and hoping to meet them. The man told me I was asking about his parents, who no longer lived in Ballisodare. I was talking to a cousin —probably several times removed, but a relative nonetheless. I asked if I could visit him, and he consented, giving me an address just outside the village.

I acquired directions from a passerby and walked down a country road through rolling green hills. I arrived at a small, well-kept, classic Irish country home with whitewashed stone walls and a thatched roof. A man maybe a couple of years older than me opened the door: my distant cousin. The poor guy had had no warning I was coming or even knowledge of my existence. It was awkward, but he graciously made me tea, and we sat there for a good half hour explaining our relations and making small talk. When he said he was in the process of studying for the bar exam, I excused myself. Bidding each other a warm goodbye, we shook hands, and I set off back to the village and Sligo town.

Back in Berkeley, my Yamaha FZ 600 motorcycle was still my sole means of transportation. For years, my friend Dan and I had talked about touring the Southwest on our bikes. During spring break of 1995, we both found ourselves with a week of free time. We packed our saddlebags, changed the oil in our bikes, and hit the road. In the next seven whirlwind days we rode 3,000 miles through four states.

The first leg of our trip was to southern California, riding through the great central valley on Interstate 5, then cutting east to Highway 99. Zipping by farms and ranches, we thrilled in the freedom. All our tools, camping gear, clothing, and other necessities were on our bikes. With nowhere in particular to be and complete mobility, we went wherever we liked. At the town of Delano, we pulled off the freeway and headed into the mountains. After winding through scrub brush canyons, we camped near Lake Isabella. The camp custodian told us about some nearby natural hot springs, so we walked there in the dark for a soak.

The next day we rode north through lower Owens Valley, farmland bordered by gargantuan mountains. Then it was a mad dash through the intense heat of Death Valley. We raced at over 100 miles per hour to get through that beautiful but harsh desert as fast as possible, stopping only to let our engines cool. As the sun went down, we crossed the state line and entered Nevada. Our muscles ached from holding position on our bikes for all those hours. Dehydrated from baking in leather jackets and helmets all day, we crested a rocky ridge. Las Vegas suddenly appeared in the valley below, looking like an alien oasis, an explosion of light and structures bursting from the desert floor. Another hour riding and we were at the apartment of an old college friend of Dan's, who let us sleep on his couches.

Me on my motorcycle in Zion National Park, 1995.

We left early the next morning, not bothering to visit the Strip or any casinos. Heading north on Interstate 15, we skirted the Great Basin. Then in Utah it was high desert and coniferous forests. Here we left the freeway and rode on a smaller road. Passing through a majestic gateway of red stone columns, we entered Zion National Park, where we camped for the night. The next day we took Highway 89 into Arizona. We passed the Grand Canyon, but by now we were short on time and couldn't stop. We continued south to Flagstaff, where we rented a room in an aged hotel.

We had to be back in the Bay Area in two days for work and were 1,000 miles from home. So the next day we rode for ten hours, covering more than 700 miles. We raced through northwest Arizona on Highway 40, quickly passing Needles and the Mojave Desert, and entered California. By this time our bikes were about as worn out as we were. Near Barstow we stopped to tighten our chains and add oil. Then back on the road for several hours until we reached Lake Isabella, where we had camped the first night of the trip. Exhausted, Dan and I slept on the ground without bothering to set up our tent.

The next day we woke up sore and aching. Fortunately our trip's last leg was short. Also, it was mostly on smooth freeway, which we welcomed by this time. In about five hours, we caught view of the San Francisco Bay. Ragged and worn but happy, Dan and I rode our luggage-laden motorcycles to the Bison to celebrate our trip's end with a handcrafted beer.

Unfortunately, shortly after this trip two of my friends died in motorcycle accidents. Julien and my mentor Paul. After that, I lost my heart for riding motorcycles. Every time I fired up the Yamaha, I thought of my dear lost friends. Also, the danger of riding was constantly in my mind. I became nervous while riding, which makes it more perilous. Soon I decided to give up motorcycles altogether. When the transmission on my FZ went out, I simply gave it away. I was sad, because I knew those free-spirited days of zooming around on two wheels were gone for good.

I spent the summer of 1997 on a cross-country road trip in a battered hand-me-down Toyota Corolla. I was more committed than ever to a career teaching capoeira, and I wanted to learn from the practices and successes, or failures, of the few teachers who were already out there. Also, I needed to scout towns and cities to decide where I would live and teach, and I had always had a Kerouacian dream of driving across the United States and back.

For three months I zigzagged across the United States and into Canada. First north to Seattle, east to Idaho, and south to Colorado. Then a long haul across the Great Plains to Chicago, Ontario, Boston, and New York. Finally it was back to California with a week of driving. In each city, I stayed with friends or relatives, and in between I camped out in national parks and forests. Wherever I could find them I visited capoeira classes, taking note of teaching methods, demographics, and levels of success.

I found two capoeira teachers in Seattle. One was a young guy teaching Capoeira Angola, the other a former student of Mestre Acordeon's named Piralito. Piralito had four or five students who trained in a Tae Kwan Do school that reminded me of Baker's Martial Arts. The Angoleiro teacher's class was about equal in size. I stayed in Boulder, Colorado, for a couple weeks, training in Galo's classes. Galo had studied under Avastruz, one of Mestre Acordeon's first students in the U.S., and had visited us in Berkeley several times. Galo seemed to be doing something right, and I was impressed by the size of his group. There were usually more than a dozen students in each class, including a handful of somewhat advanced students. This made it a relatively large and advanced group for the U.S. in those days.

In Chicago I took a class led by Marisa, a Brazilian woman. In Boston, Mestre Deraldo, an established Angola teacher. In New York, Mestre Jelon, the first capoeira teacher in the U.S. Also in New York I attended a demonstration and seminar held by Mestre Itaopoan, a student of Mestre Bimba. This was where I first met Mestre Efraim, a warm and gregarious man whom I would encounter many more times over the years.

Driving across the continent and back, I saw Yellowstone National Park, Niagara Falls, Mount Rainier, and the Great Plains. I camped in the Rocky Mountains, the Utah desert, and the forests of upstate New York. My many roads included the I-5 North, the 80 East, Route 1 South, and Route 50, known as the Loneliest Road in America. I traveled over 7,000 miles coast-to-coast before rolling back into Berkeley in the little old Toyota.

# CHAPTER ELEVEN

# Brazil

Dreadlocks flying, Dondi stepped forward and spun around to face us. He wore his usual smile, but his tone was grim. "Okay folks, it's time to play some capoeira. Who's down?"

Dondi was the leader of our United Capoeira Association sister group in Tucson, Arizona. It was 1999, in the city of São Salvador, Bahia, Brazil. We were part of a group of about fifty Americans, led by Mestre Rã. Mestre Acordeon would join us soon.

Capoeira Brazil, a large group with branches in many different countries, was holding its annual gathering that weekend in Bahia. Tonight's event was a big roda in a hall to which we had just arrived for a visit. The music had started and the jogos were about to begin, but we Americans hung back near the entrance. I think we felt intimidated by an intense atmosphere, and a lack of warmth from our hosts. Mestre Jelon was there, and he and Mestre Rã greeted each other civilly enough. But most of the rest of the people, big, athletic youths, seemed like they viewed our arrival as intrusive, if anything.

When the games began, they were instantly physical and rough. On the second or third game, somebody was swept on to their back. In the next game there was an exchange of hard kicks to the body. A few minutes later, two players ended up grappling on the floor. Everyone was fierce, men and women alike, and played to dominate.

Seeing this state of affairs and concerned that our group might not represent in this roda at all, Dondi had spoken up.

After an awkward pause, Boi responded. "I'll go." He was one of the oldest and least experienced capoeiristas in our group. He stepped forward and stood by Dondi.

I felt afraid, but Dondi and Boi had snapped me out of it. "I'm ready," I said. "Let's go." I stepped to Dondi's side.

Dondi, Boi, and I looked back at our group, waiting for others to join us. Nobody stepped forward.

"That's it? Come on guys, let's get in that roda and represent!" Dondi exclaimed. Turning to some of our upper-level students, he urged them forward.

"Oh no, I'm not getting in there," we heard. "Umm, no thanks." Some quietly looked at the ground, refusing to make eye contact.

Throwing up his hands in disgust, Dondi turned to Boi and me. "Well, I guess it's just us, guys. Let's do this." We left the group and approached the pé do berimbau.

As we squeezed through the crowd, the intensity level rose even higher. The music was increasing in tempo, and several people were slammed on the ground by a takedown or knocked out by a kick. Mestre Rã played a huge, powerful, aggressive man, and for the first time I saw him struggle to hold his own. Even reaching the front of the line to get in the roda was a battle. We jostled and elbowed our way forward through sweaty bodies.

Dondi led the way into the roda and played his game. Still with a smile, Dondi faked, feinted, dodged, and kicked for a good thirty seconds before a vingativa sweep took him down. Then it was my turn. I faced the young man squatting across from me. He might have been no more than eighteen years old, but almost a foot taller than me, and muscular. As I offered my hand to shake, he gave me a dismissive glance. We both did a quick *a ú* into the roda. I stayed low and grounded, determined not to be swept off my feet.

*My game in the Capoeira Brazil roda, Mestre Jelon in background, Bahia, Brazil, 1999.*

Stepping, kicking, and dodging, I avoided acrobatics, as I knew my opponent would make short work of me if I gave him an opening. He let fly a few high, distant kicks that were only probes of my defenses and not true attacks. As I did a spinning armada kick, he deftly passed underneath and emerged suddenly at my side, occupying the coveted center of the roda and taking the advantage. Now my back was against the circle's edge, and I had less room to maneuver. I knew he had me cornered but tried to push him back or escape to the side.

The guy was too quick and big, though, and wouldn't budge or let me gain any ground, cutting off my every move. As he swung back into a crouch, I sensed what was coming. I searched for a way out, but I couldn't dodge fast enough when he sprang at me. His flying chapa kick hit me in the ribs, projecting me up off my feet. I flew backward, over the people sitting at the roda's edge, and landed on my back outside the circle. I sprang to my feet, ready to continue the jogo. But the game was over, and Boi was already playing one of the Brazilians. I brushed myself off and attempted to recover my dignity as I watched Boi get similarly pushed around.

Eventually a few other Americans entered the roda, to pretty much the same results. As we left, we spoke little. I wasn't happy with my game and being kicked out of the roda. But I was proud at least a few of us had played that night, thanks to Dondi. Perhaps we had been humbled, but at least we had shown Capoeira Brazil we had the courage to get in the roda with them.

My first trip to Brazil had been in 1993, with Mestre Rã and ten other students. It was then I had first received my nickname, Galego. We had been in São Paulo at Mestre Suassuna's academy, where the capoeira was amazing, with explosively acrobatic games the norm and music on point. Mestre Suassuna, famous for creating the Miudinho style and for his many excellent music albums, is also known for his stinging wit. Galego literally means Galician, i.e., people of Galicia, the Celtic province of Northwest Spain. But galegos are often the butt of jokes in Brazil, similar to how blonds, various ethnic groups, or anyone, can be targets of people not like them. I don't remember what I did, but it was typically awkward or uncoordinated, and Mestre Suassuna made a galego joke about me. I liked the nickname, though, because of my Celtic ancestry.

On that trip, we went to Mestre Rã's hometown of Jundiai. At his student's school, I accidentally knocked out a guy with a *meia lua de compasso* kick. I felt horrible, but maybe karma is real because six years later the same kick knocked me out in the same town.

I went on group trips with one or both of our mestres in 1993, 1999, 2002, and 2004. Each trip followed roughly the same itinerary, including São Paulo, Rio de Janeiro, and Salvador, Bahia. Rio is notable for its sights, including many lovely beaches and Corcovado Mountain, where the massive Jesus Christ the Redeemer statue looks over the city. In Rio we visited the classes of Mestre Peixinho, Mestre Ramos, and Mestre Gato, renowned masters and founders of the group Capoeira Senzala. The capoeira here was less flashy and more combative than what we had seen in São Paulo.

*Aú sem mão in a roda in São Paulo, Brazil, 2003.*

Most of the trips ended in Salvador, Bahia. This area is the cradle of African Brazilian culture, steeped in music, dance, history, and a rich cultural tradition. It sits on the northern side of a large natural bay, the Bahia de Todos Santos. Salvador's many beaches line the Atlantic Ocean, reaching to Africa, the ancestral motherland to so many of Bahia's residents. At the tip of land where the coast meets the bay, a massive *farol*, or lighthouse, stands on a fortress.

As the bay curves inland, the land rises to a high bluff. Between the water and the bluff's cliffside is Cidade Baixa, the Low City. This is home to docks, warehouses, and the famous Mercado Modelo, Model Market, built over the old slave catacombs. Atop the bluff is the Cidade Alta, the High City. This area includes the downtown and the historic Pelorinho district, home of the famed samba reggae music group Olodum and Mestre Bimba's old academy, where legends were born.

*With Mestre Lobão on berimbau, São Paulo, 2003.*

One time our group took a boat trip from Salvador across the Bay to Itaparica Island, a favorite getaway of Bahians.

We chartered a medium-sized longboat with sails and tall masts—although it used a motor for propulsions. As we prepared to leave the island, the weather suddenly changed from sunny to dark and cloudy. By the time we boarded our boat, it was raining hard, and as we set off across the bay, a strong wind came up. Soon we could no longer see the bay's far side, or much in any direction. Wind whipped around us and drove waves against the side of our boat. Sheets of rain soaked everything and everyone above deck. We grew nervous as the storm worsened and we saw the crew's concerned expressions.

*From left, Mestre Acordeon, me, Mestre Ramos, Mestre Gato, Professor Dondi (behind), Professor Galo, and Mestre Peixinho, Rio de Janeiro, 2003.*

Waves heightened, and the boat rocked more and more. My stomach couldn't take it, and I joined several others vomiting over the boat's side. Seeking respite, many of us went below to the cabins. The engines blew noxious fumes into the interior, however, increasing our nausea and worry. A few Americans became panicky and somebody started to cry. Unable to see where we were or where we were headed, rain-soaked and battered by gale force winds and monster waves, I think we were all worried.

Finally the wind let up and the rain relented. The waves calmed, the sky brightened, and we began to think we would be okay. The sun appeared as we came within sight of Salvador's docks. As the boat was moored to the pier, we disembarked with relief. Our fears of a watery death now seemed ridiculous, and we laughed at how frightened we had been.

*Mestre Boa Gente, me, Mestre Acordeon, Bahia, 2004.*

After 2004 I didn't manage to get back to Brazil until 2013, when I took a small group of my students there. This time, for a change, we went to Recife and Paraiba in the far Northeast, as well as to Bahia and Rio. Although I wasn't able to give my students the amazing experience in Brazil my mestres had given me, they still had a good time, and it made me proud to introduce them to friends like Mestre Boa Gente, Mestre Nenel, and Mestre Gato.

One day back in Berkeley after the 1999 trip, Mestre Acordeon and Mestre Rã called me into their office.

Mestre Rã spoke first. "Galego, how are you feeling?"

"Fine, Mestre. I'm feeling good."

"How do you feel your training is going?" Mestre Acordeon peered intently at my face as he always did when he asked a question.

I responded cautiously, wanting to seem neither overly confident nor insecure. "I think it is going well, Mestre. I know there are many things I can still improve on, but at this point I feel my game and knowledge are decent."

Mestre Acordeon looked slightly doubtful about my assessment, but then again he seldom seemed entirely happy with his students' responses.

"Do you know why we asked you in here?" asked Mestre Rã.

"Um, no. I don't."

Mestre Rã continued. "You've been training for about nine years now, right?"

"That's right."

"You've been doing well. We've seen you improve a lot over the years. You've trained a lot, and traveled and visited many rodas and other schools."

"Thank you, Mestre."

Mestre Acordeon spoke. "Galego, we've decided to move you up this year. At this batizado we are going to have your *formatura*." He paused to see my reaction. Formatura meant graduation.

For a moment I was at a loss for words. I had known this day would eventually come, but still I was surprised. "Wow, Mestre. Thank you," I said simply.

"What do you think?" Mestre Rã asked.

I paused again, attempting to recall my thoughts on the subject. The formatura would be my graduation from capoeira school. With it would come the authorization to start and teach my own group.

Finally I said, "Mestres, thank you so much for your recognition. I'm happy you think I am ready to graduate. I would be honored to do so, but the truth is I don't think I'm ready. The thing is, after my formatura, I plan to move immediately to Sacramento to start a group there. Before I do that, I want to be really well prepared. I want to speak Portuguese, have a better game, and know more about all the music and arts related to capoeira."

Now it was the mestres who appeared to be at a loss for words. I continued, "If it's okay with both of you, can we postpone my formatura until next year? I'd like the chance to train more and go to Brazil again."

Now my mestres looked pleased. In his low, deliberate voice, Mestre Acordeon said, "Okay, Galego. I think that is a good idea. What do you think, Mestre Rã?"

Mestre Rã looked at Mestre Acordeon and then at me. "I think it's a good idea too. Okay, Galego, we will put off your formatura until next year."

I thanked them and left the office. I had one year to prepare for graduation, so I quickly planned another trip to Brazil.

# CHAPTER TWELVE

# Brazil Redux

The year 2000 dawned and, contrary to the belief of some an apocalypse didn't ensue. Christian fundamentalists said 2000 would be the beginning of the "end-times," new-agers predicted environmental disaster or extraterrestrial visitation, and even the secular feared the Y2K bug. The Y2K bug was going to crash computer systems worldwide on January 1, 2000, leading to chaos and destruction. People were stockpiling supplies, finishing their bucket lists, and building underground bunkers. I packed my bags for a to return to Brazil, this time for an extended stay.

Two friends from capoeira school, Christina and Nikia, were also going to Brazil, so we decided to travel together. We caught a flight to Rio in January of 2000 with a vague plan to first spend a week in Rio. Then we would travel by bus to the state of Bahia, where Mestre Suassuna was hosting a weeklong capoeira event called Capoeirando. This is a big annual event with teachers and students from all over the world gathering for a week of workshops, rodas, performances, and festivities. It was a focal point of our trip and one of our few concrete plans. In the meantime, upon arriving in Rio, we needed a place to stay and a way to spend our time. Our Lonely Planet travel guide helped us find a cheap hotel in the Lapa neighborhood.

After a few days in Rio, we caught a bus north to Bahia. It was a long, complicated journey just navigating to the *rodoviária*, the interstate bus hub found in every major town. Luckily Christina spoke Portuguese well and received quality directions. When we finally found the rodoviária, we discovered the bus trip to Bahia was thirty-six hours! The payoff was that it only cost about 90 *reals*, the Brazilian currency. At four reals to the U.S. dollar, this was just $22. We boarded the bus and settled down for the long ride.

The bus would have been comfortable if it hadn't been so cold. I don't know why interstate Brazilian buses are generally kept at freezing temperatures. Perhaps the bus proprietors like to show off their air conditioners, or maybe since Brazil is so hot most of the time, Brazilians like to get their coldness when they can. In any case, we were unprepared for the chill and spent a day and a half shivering in our seats.

Disembarking in the small town of Itacaré on Bahia's southern coast, Nikia, Christina, and I were glad to emerge into the tropical environment. Locals gave us directions to Mestre Suassuna's property a few kilometers down the road. We caught a bus, which thankfully lacked air conditioning, then walked the last stretch down a country lane, hoping we were in the right place. Soon we came upon a gate. The word "Capoeirando" was scrawled in spray paint across a big piece of plywood.

We spent the next week camping at the property, several beautiful acres of beachfront coconut groves. There were about a dozen permanent residents on site, a few dozen Brazilian capoeiristas, and a cadre of teachers who taught scheduled classes every day. Every morning, noon, and night, we trained capoeira on a concrete slab or at another nearby site that looked like an abandoned school. The teachers included the founder of the Cordão de Ouro group, Mestre Suassuna; Mestre Jogo de Dentro, a leading teacher of the Capoeira Angola style in Bahia; Mestre Bimba's son Mestre Nenel; Mestre Urubu, who we knew from the Bay Area; Mestre Lobão, a great master from the São Paulo area, and many more. There were maybe one hundred and fifty capoeiristas from many different countries. We ran into several people from our Berkeley school, including Marreta, Espanta Leão, and Pincel.

There was at least one roda after most workshops and again at the end of the day, always packed with people and buzzing with energy. I tried to play a lot, but as I had found at many Brazilian rodas, it was a battle just to enter the circle. Crowds of sweaty capoeiristas pressed all around, forming a solid wall. I had to pry my way through just to get within sight of the action. Then, after I had slowly progressed toward the front of the line, my knees aching from staying in the mandatory squatting position, some talented kid would simply cut in front of me. Finally I would get a turn and try to work some circulation into my legs as I shook a stranger's hand.

The pace was frenetic, the music pulsing, and the roda tiny. The game was a blur as I attempted to maneuver and complete a few of my best moves while dodging dangerous kicks. Then, just as I would feel I might be loosening up and on the verge of doing something good, someone would buy into the game and cut me out. In an instant it was all over, and I was back outside of the roda, wondering if I should bother with the whole process again or forget it and go to the beach.

In between workshops and rodas, we washed off sweat in the ocean surf. This was sometimes the only bathing available, as the whole compound had only one shower stall. Each night after the last class and roda, there was a long samba de roda session or *forró* dancing at a nearby café. Then we wearily walked to our tents to sleep, waking a few short hours later to start again.

When the week was over, we left Mestre Suassuna's property with bittersweet relief and headed for town. Every inch of our bodies was tired and sore, and we could hardly wait to find a hotel and take a real shower.

After a night in a little sun-bleached hotel in Itacaré, we took a bus northward to Salvador. Passing through Bahia's coastal area, or *litoral*, we enjoyed a beautiful landscape of lush tropical forests, white-sand beaches, rolling hills, and quaint small towns characterized by colonial architecture. When we finally rolled into the rodoviária of Salvador, the urban cacophony stunned our country-conditioned senses. The din of roaring vehicles, hawkers selling wares, loudspeakers blaring music and promotions, and thousands of people talking and bustling about, blasted us as we got off the bus. Pausing to find our bearings and recover from the shock, we consulted our trusty guidebook. We decided to find a cheap *pousada*, an inn, in the Barra neighborhood, and walked across a freeway overpass to catch a local bus.

I had two types of bus experiences in Brazil. Interstate buses and the upscale executivo local buses offered plush, cushioned seats with plenty of legroom. They often provided a television or two set up high, showing the news or popular novellas, soap operas. These more luxurious rides were, of course, more expensive. And, as previously mentioned, the air conditioners were consistently on full blast.

The local city buses were entirely different. These were by far the more common buses in Brazil, frequented by the great majority of Brazilians for all manner of daily transport. These contraptions of mass conveyance generally bore the scars of many years' service and were expressions of frugality. No unnecessary cushions adorned those hard-framed bucket seats. The temperature matched the air outside or was hotter because of all the bodies pressed together.

On these buses, I witnessed drama, romance, small livestock animals, and occasionally people with gruesome medical conditions exposed for all to see. City buses served the poor, prostitutes, transvestites, con men, beggars, pickpockets, street performers, Bible thumpers, and more. One time, a troop of local boys boarded my bus, taking over the last couple rows of seats. As they streamed down the center aisle, they sang a popular song, and when they took their seats, they tapped the beat on the seats in front of them.

This progressed into a batucada, Brazilian drum corps, jam. They used every surface within reach as an instrument and various objects as drumsticks. They were quite skilled, shifting into a spirited and complex samba reggae jam session complete with syncopated beats and coordinated breaks in the music. As the other riders and I bobbed our heads in time with the impromptu concert, a young lady rose from her seat and danced in the aisle. The bus was transformed into a live music dance party. Then the bus stopped at the boys' destination, and they clambered out to the street, taking their music with them.

Christina, Nikia, and I arrived in Barra's familiar surroundings. We left the bus near the lighthouse and walked through a bright, cheery neighborhood. After viewing a couple dubious looking pousadas, we settled on a charming if modest establishment called Pousada Ambar. Newly built, this place had colorful décor, an open-air courtyard, friendly young employees, and affordable communal bunk-rooms. It was comfortable and secure, and we made several friends and contacts there. Just a few days after we showed up, a couple of the Brazilians who worked there befriended us. They were cheerful, young *Bahianos*, eager to practice their English and happy to show us around.

We also met John and Ruari, a couple of fun-loving Australian guys who were slowly touring South America. They were passing time at the Ambar while waiting for an apartment they were going to rent. Along with some other friends, they would stay through *Carnaval*, the famously bacchanalian festival soon to occur in Bahia's streets and all across Brazil. Their apartment had extra space, so they invited us to join them there. We had no plans for where to stay and what to do during Carnaval, so we happily accepted the invitation.

The next week, we moved into the apartment, a large space with several bedrooms a few blocks from the Porto da Barra beach. There was no furniture, so we bought foam pads at a local hardware store: our beds for the next month. We Americans shared one bedroom, Ruari and John shared another, and we reserved the third for the Australians' friend who would arrive later. Additional friends would rent the living room during the week of Carnaval. The kitchen was adequate, and large windows looked out from the third floor to the busy street below.

There were still a couple of weeks until Carnaval, so we had plenty of time to prepare for this party of all parties. I enrolled in an intensive two-week Portuguese course and attended class every morning, learning vocabulary, grammar, and pronunciation at a feverish pace. When not in class, I eagerly practiced with Brazilians around town. It was fun and rewarding to have conversations in Portuguese, but it was also frustrating and sometimes embarrassing.

Confusing similar words, or even emphasizing the wrong syllable, could result in disaster. One time I meant to ask a street vendor for a *coco verde*, a green coconut drink. Instead, I asked for a *cocô verde*, a green shit drink. Then there was the time I went to a department store to buy some new clothes. When I asked the attendant where to find men's t-shirts, I confused the word *camisetas*, t-shirts, with *camisinhas*, condoms. He politely informed me they did not sell condoms.

As Carnaval approached, the heightened energy throughout the city was palpable. From our apartment windows we watched a steady stream of people travel in the same direction. They came from the inland hills to the seaside, where the main party would happen. Many of the smaller streets that met the main boulevard had been closed to traffic and transformed into ramshackle party zones dotted with hastily constructed *barracas*, small huts. These stands sold all manner of food and drink, including mixed drinks, beer, meat kabobs grilled over an open flame, and *acaraje*, dumplings made from cassava root flour and deep fried in palm oil. We eagerly explored these chaotic street fairs and sampled the offerings.

On the first day of Carnaval, revelers filled the streets. I walked to the beach with Christina and Ruari for a midday swim, marveling at the transformation that had occurred. Large temporary structures stood on the sidewalk and sections of the beach bordering the boulevard. These stands contained bleachers and luxury boxes for viewing the procession to come. In some sections, these temporary buildings were so tall on both sides of the street that they created a kind of man-made canyon. Everywhere the barracas sold their food, juices, and alcohol, unregulated by the laws and restrictions we were used to in the U.S. Throngs of people were all about, often bursting into spontaneous dance sessions when a popular song blasted on somebody's sound system. We were told this was still the warm-up; the real party would start after sundown.

Our group assembled back at the apartment to discuss strategy. We decided that before making any serious decisions, we should start with a round of *caipirinhas*. It was my turn to make them, and I focused on making our first drink of Carnaval a good one.

After sipping our caipirinhas and considering the reports of Carnaval veterans, we settled on a plan. Go into the street, have some more drinks in the barracas down the street, and then make our way to the boulevard where the *trio elétricos* would parade. Ruari and John explained what a trio elétrico was, but I wouldn't really understand until I saw one. After joining Carnaval proper, we would wander at will but stay in groups of two or three for safety's sake.

Ruari, John, Christina, Nikia, and I made our way onto the street, the caipirinha buzz augmenting the high we were getting from the mass excitement around us. So many people, Brazilian and international, full of joy and exuberance. It was clear that for many, this was a highlight of the year, preceded by months of preparation and anticipation.

As we approached the main boulevard, we heard the crowd's din, which grew steadily as the sun began to set. We stopped at a barraca, one we visited nightly as our prelude to the main event. The proprietor, a jovial middle-aged man named Victor, made us some strong *kapetas*, a mixed drink with the ubiquitous *cachaça* liquor, condensed milk, cocoa, and guarana powder. A plant native to Brazil, guarana's seeds contain about twice the caffeine of coffee beans, making it a powerful stimulant. Guarana powder is common in juice drinks, the frozen sorbet-like desert açai, and alcoholic beverages. Needless to say, the concoction further amped our buzz.

Ruari was our unofficial leader and guide. We newbies were eager to approach the boulevard, but he suggested taking it slow. "It's going to be a long night, my friends. Let's pace ourselves and enjoy another drink here before we get caught up in the storm."

Ever amiable, Christina agreed. "Good idea, Ruari. I'll have another kapeta."

I was impatient, as usual. "Come on, guys. Don't you want to get over there?" The commotion was rising on the boulevard.

Ruari smiled at me. "Patience, my Yank friend. The trios haven't even started yet."

Victor concurred. "*Paciência amigos. Fica aqui comigo um pouco mais.*"

I reluctantly agreed and bought another kapeta.

By now our host Victor had come to know us enough to assign most of us nicknames. With his blond locks and Hawaiian shirt, Ruari was "Surfista." I was "Olhos de Gato," in reference to my green eyes. Victor joked around with us and offered a few tips, communicating mainly through Christina, who had the best Portuguese. Stick together and don't wander alone, he urged us. Leave whenever a *briga*, a fight, breaks out. When the police pass through the crowd, get out of their way. His final words of advice were for each of us to find ourselves a *gatinha* o r *gatinho,* a term for attractive young women and men, for a *beijinho*, a little kiss.

Fortified by alcohol, caffeine, and a veteran Brazilian carnavilista's wisdom, we left the barraca and walked eagerly to the boulevard. Finally—Carnaval!

Turning the corner from the side street into the large open area where the boulevard met the farol, we met with a spectacular sight. Massive crowds of people pulsed with energy and excitement. About one hundred yards up the boulevard, an explosion of light and sound slowly rumbled toward us. It was an eighteen-wheel freight truck rigged with a huge sound system and a stage on top, where a band was playing with mad abandon. Blazing light displays turned the whole area as bright as day. This was a trio elétrico, accompanied by a horde of dancers. The mass of people slowly passed by us.

We stood frozen in amazement. The spectacle was unlike anything I had ever seen. But a contagious urge to join in the revelry washed away any intimidation. Glancing at each other, we saw the same glee and anticipation on each other's faces. As another trio elétrico passed by, we jumped into the fray as if into the ocean's crashing surf. We danced and played as waves of people swept us to and fro.

That night we danced and walked for miles, following trios up the boulevard along the sea, then returning to where we had started to catch another one. We broke into pairs and threes, rejoined, drank, talked, and separated again. Strangers grabbed us, dancing wildly with us before disappearing into the crowd. Losing ourselves in the abandon and celebration, we caught the fever of Carnaval's mass, frenzied joy.

By the time weak tendrils of light began to reach across the sky, we were exhausted and footsore but elated and still reluctant to go home. We sat for a time on the wall bordering the beach, talking about the night. Drowsy, half-drunk, too tired to keep going, and too excited to stop, we lazily laughed at each other's stories. Finally, as the sun broke above the horizon, we walked back to the apartment and slumped onto our beds for a sound sleep.

Later that day, after five or six hours' rest, we woke and walked to the beach for a swim. Returning to our apartment, we ate and prepared for another night out, then gathered for a round of caipirinhas and started all over again. Once again we stayed out all night dancing, drinking, and cavorting through the streets of Bahia. In the morning we returned to the apartment, exhausted and happy. We continued this routine for a week, celebrating each day like there was no tomorrow, along with several million Brazilians and people from around the world.

During the six weeks in Salvador we hadn't trained capoeira at all. Most of the capoeira schools shut down or cut back their programs during Carnaval season, and we were preoccupied anyway. Still, I learned a lot during this time that helped my capoeira, including Portuguese language, dance, and music. But now that Carnaval was over, I wanted to return to training.

*Carnaval, Filhos de Gandhi group, Bahia, 2000.*

I had met a master called Mestre Espirro Mirim at a capoeira encounter in San Francisco. This wiry athlete was incredibly skilled, doing seemingly impossible flips and contortions and lightning-speed kicks. He was part of the Cordão de Ouro group and lived in the northern city of Fortaleza, where he taught at his own school. Although I didn't have its phone number or address, I would head north to find it.

Christina was heading north to visit a friend in Natal, so we traveled together. Nikia's trip was at its end, and she was headed back to the U.S. Our Australian friends would stay in Salvador for a few months, so we planned to meet up when our paths crossed again.

Our bus ride was another long, freezing journey. After about thirty hours, we arrived in Natal, a small city on the coast near Brazil's northeastern-most tip. This beautiful area is known for endless white sand beaches and a lively cultural arts scene, including lots of capoeira and the dances of forró and *frevo*.

I spent the next couple of weeks exploring gorgeous beaches, spending time with Christina and her friend Thais, and visiting local capoeira schools. Here, away from the major metropolitan areas and capoeira super-schools, the capoeira groups were not so different from those in the U.S. The mestre was the teacher and organizer, enforcing standards of conduct and reasonable behavior in class and roda. Classes included one or two top-level students with excellent physical skills, several medium-level students, and a bunch of beginners. As usual, Brazilian groups had fewer female capoeiristas than I saw in the U.S., but there were usually at least a couple in each group. These visits provided great opportunities to learn from different teachers and play many different capoeiristas.

Thais took us two hours south to a tiny fishing village in a remote area of the coast. We stayed at her surfer friend's place, an open-air hut beside the sea. That night we walked up a hill to a house larger than the rest. There, the village was holding a forró party with live music and dancing. A trio of musicians belted out tunes while a half-dozen or so couples swayed and twirled on the open floor. When the villagers saw us, the only foreigners around, they welcomed us heartily. When they found out I had never danced forró, they took it upon themselves to educate me. I think I danced with every villager there, man and woman.

Soon it was time for me to continue on my journey to Fortaleza, and I said a sad goodbye to Christina as I boarded another bus. This time the ride was only twenty hours. I arrived in Fortaleza midmorning and disembarked, disoriented with little knowledge of the area.

After finding a budget hotel a few blocks from the beach, I spent the next week searching for Mestre Espirro's classes, asking random individuals if they knew of him or any other capoeira. In the meantime, I ran a few miles each day and trained capoeira on the beach. I didn't know anybody in Fortaleza, and most of the Brazilians there spoke little English, so I got to practice my Portuguese a lot.

Eventually someone told me about a local capoeira class, and the teacher at that class gave me a phone number and address for Mestre Espirro. The object of my quest remained elusive, however, as the phone number connected me with a lady who had no idea what I was talking about. I set out for the address, taking a bus to the other side of town as my hotel owner indicated. I left in the afternoon, hoping there would be a class that night and giving myself plenty of time to find the location.

After several transfers and laborious conversations for directions, I landed in what I hoped was the class's vicinity. I showed the address to a passerby who directed me to what looked like a high school. It was early evening, and the campus appeared deserted, but I entered anyway.

The complex felt empty and lifeless as I walked among darkened buildings. It was kind of creepy, and I began to feel nervous. I was about to give up and conclude my lead had been false when faintly and from a distance, I heard a familiar twang. It was unmistakable—the sound of a berimbau!

Following the sound, I entered a dark hallway. The music grew louder, and I heard voices as well. I turned a corner and saw light at the end of a passage. Soon I was pleased to find a large gymnasium full of capoeiristas. At the far end were several people playing instruments, including Mestre Espirro on *pandeiro*. I had found him!

After introducing myself I joined the class, beginning with a partner sequence. It was complex, involving various attacks, defenses, and groundwork, and it took me a while to catch on. Then it was time for a different drill with a new partner. It was a takedown, and my partner slammed me to the ground on the first repetition.

Toward the end of class, Mestre Espirro called everyone together for a roda. He introduced me as Mestre Acordeon's student and representative, which was generous of him and an honor for me. The music started at a fast tempo. Two people entered the circle for the first game, and my eyes widened as they both opened with fantastically high flips. After that all the games were fast and intense. This capoeira was exceptionally high-level, with a degree of athleticism and skill I had not seen since Capoeirando. I played several times and struggled to keep up. I learned that many of these people were *professors* or *contramestres* (upper-level teachers). These were Mestre Espirro's graduated students who continued to train with him on a regular basis. The technical training and high level of capoeira was what I needed. I was excited to practice here as much as possible.

Mestre Espirro held class three times a week, and I attended each class during the rest of my stay in Fortaleza. The training was demanding physically and mentally, testing and increasing my speed and endurance. New techniques and concepts expanded my understanding and skills.

One long sequence I liked combined Mestre Bimba's seqüências with the cintura desprezada and several other *balões*, acrobatic partner throws. Each of the traditional seqüências changed to conclude with one of the throws. I would teach this sequence to my own students many years later. On the nights Mestre Espirro did not have class, I usually visited the class of one of his students, who taught in various locations around the city. After several weeks of this routine, my body was toned and my capoeira sharp.

The date of my flight back to the U.S. from Rio approached, and I hit the road again, this time south. Taking the bus back to Natal, I spent a few days visiting Christina. Then I continued on to Bahia, where I stayed at the same apartment with John and Ruari. Then I had about one more week in that magical city.

As before, we usually went to the Porto da Barra beach during the day and out in the Pelorinho at night. It was at the beach one day that I met a beautiful African-Brazilian woman with a confident bearing. She and I had exchanged glances, and I took the unusually bold step, for me, of approaching her directly.

"Good afternoon," I wished her in Portuguese with a smile.

She replied in kind.

"My name is Patrick. What is your name?" I continued, still in Portuguese and keeping it simple.

"Marta."

"It's a pleasure." I shook her hand.

"A pleasure," she replied, also in Portuguese. "Where are you from?"

"I'm from the United States. And you?"

At this she laughed, and smiled at me for the first time. It was stunning.

"I'm from here. I am Bahiana!" she declared proudly.

We talked for a while longer and made plans to go out that night. A few hours later we met at a restaurant for dinner, and then went to a bar where we danced to the *Axé* music so popular in Bahia. As we said goodbye at the end of the evening, we shared a passionate kiss and agreed to see each other the next day.

Over the next couple weeks Marta and I progressed through a whirlwind romance, getting carried away with excitement. I was impressed with her strength of character and courageous attitude. She dreamed of a career teaching the dance of her native Bahia in a foreign land. Her dreams paralleled, if conversely, my own plans of a career teaching foreign arts in my native land. She seemed willing to take a risk to make her dream come true, as was I for mine. I told her of my passion for capoeira and intention to pursue a career teaching it. She liked the idea.

I considered the drastic idea of inviting Marta to Sacramento to partner with me in my mission to teach capoeira. I understood that we barely knew each other, but the potential of us working together and combining our complementary skills seemed powerful. I could teach capoeira, and she could teach African Brazilian dance, a natural pairing. I could facilitate her visit and help her become a U.S. resident. We would be allies and partners. I already knew Marta had thought about leaving Bahia. She was prepared to start a new life in an unknown city, which was what I was preparing to do myself.

There were only a few days until I had to leave Bahia, and I had to make a decision. I confided my idea to a few people, most of whom told me I was crazy. Surely I couldn't expect someone I barely knew to drop everything and to join me in the U.S.. Ignoring conventional wisdom, I decided talk to Marta about it anyway.

In broken Portuguese, I laid out my proposal to Marta. I explained I thought we could be good partners. Maybe we could even help each other make our dreams come true. I described Sacramento and my plan to move there. She could teach samba, and together we could create a powerful program. Yes, we didn't know each other well, and I admitted it was a risky plan. But she would get a roundtrip plane ticket, and if things didn't work out she could always return to Bahia.

Marta was intrigued. She had family and friends in Bahia, but career opportunities weren't there. She dreamed of a life in the U.S., but it also terrified her to think of everything that could go wrong. She asked questions about Sacramento, my plans, how we would make money, and a lot of other things. I answered to the best of my ability, but some things I still didn't know myself.

Eventually Marta said she was interested in my proposal but needed time to think about it. I promised that if she took this leap of faith, I would be there to catch her.

On my final day in Bahia I met with Marta. I didn't want to convince or pressure her, but we were out of time, so I asked her directly, "Marta, will you go to the United States with me? For us to live and work together?"

She sighed and remained quiet for a long moment. Finally she looked into my eyes and nodded. "*Vou.*"

I was stunned. "Yes?"

"*Sim, eu vou, eu vou.*" We both smiled broadly. I felt excited, surprised, happy, and nervous, and I know she must have felt the same things. Struggling to think and communicate clearly, we made a rough plan for her to apply for a U.S. visa and join me a few months later.

I said goodbye for now to Marta and my other friends in Bahia. One more long bus ride got me to Rio, and gave me plenty of time to think about what had been set in motion. So many things could go wrong including with Marta getting a visa, her reaction to life in California, and where our relationship might lead. But I was elated with the grand possibilities that our union had the potential for. Working together, the two of us could accomplish much more than we could alone. It certainly wouldn't be easy, but Marta coming to the U.S. might catapult both of us onto the field of our dreams.

# PART THREE

# Teach

## CHAPTER THIRTEEN

# A New Beginning

Back from Brazil, I was once again teaching gymnastics and training capoeira. Our U.C.A batizado and formatura were coming up, and I was scheduled to graduate. After the formatura, I would move to Sacramento and start building a teaching career. I would be one of only a handful of North American graduated capoeira teachers. I was in top shape, and immersion in Brazil had deeply improved my Portuguese, music, dance, and understanding of the culture. This time, I was ready.

Marta and I communicated by email as she applied for a visa, and I prepared to move to Sacramento in August, uncertain if she would come along. I called gymnastics schools in Sacramento looking for a job. With a great reference from Head Over Heels, I was offered a part-time coaching position that would start upon my arrival. I called Mathew, an old friend from the Bison days and the only person I knew in Sacramento. He ran a café and happened to have a bedroom opening up in the house he rented. He invited me to take it, and I agreed. The bare necessities were in place for this next stage of life.

Lacking experience in entrepreneurship, I made up a business plan as I went along. After hours, I used the computers at work to make promotional pamphlets and flyers. I used my own material in all my public relations, never borrowing outside photos or artwork. A couple of volunteers from the capoeira academy joined me for a promotional photoshoot with my cheap cameras. In one of these photos, I am in a handstand and Cravo is doing a *cabeçada* (head butt), which eventually became the figures in my business logo.

I discussed my plan with Mestre Acordeon and Mestre Rã. Mestre Rã encouraged me enthusiastically. Mestre Acordeon encouraged me as well, but also asked hard questions about my research into the Sacramento market, my business plan, my relationship with Marta, and how we would sustain ourselves while building a business. I answered to the best of my ability, and he seemed cautiously satisfied.    His questioning helped me prepare for the difficulties to come.

Mestre Acordeon gave me the phone numbers of two people in Sacramento who were interested in capoeira. Magen, whom we called Caxias, had seen some of our group's students playing capoeira in a park and had asked them about it. They had taken her number and given it to Mestre Acordeon. A guy named Dom had asked Mestre Acordeon to send somebody to Sacramento to teach capoeira. I called them both and told them I would soon be on my way.

Early in June, Marta told me she had been granted a visa and would come to California. This was it—we were going to do it! On the day of her arrival, I bought a bouquet of flowers on the way to the airport. I still felt unsure that she would actually appear. She would be so far out of her comfort zone. I would do my best to care for her and help her adapt to the U.S.

I waited anxiously at the gate in the airport. Her flight arrived, and people began streaming in. I did not see her, and as the flow of passengers dwindled, so did my hope. Suddenly she appeared, almost the last person to leave the plane. She looked around cautiously. She walked with her typical proud bearing, but signs of weariness and worry showed on her face. When she saw me, her body relaxed, and she flashed me her stunning smile. I pressed the flowers into her hands and hugged her. She had made it—we were in it together now.

A few weeks later Cravo and I graduated from our capoeira academy. The academy was packed with students and teachers from all over the world. As usual, Mestre Acordeon was the master of ceremonies, and he took his time eloquently guiding the proceedings. First there were introductions of all the mestres and other guest teachers, followed by a teachers' roda where they displayed their awesome skills. After that was the batizado when dozens of new students received their first cordão after playing one of the mestres. Then came the *troca de cordões*, when each level of students received promotion to the next cord. Late in the afternoon, it was time for Cravo and me to graduate.

Our formatura was quick and to the point. Mestre Acordeon made a brief speech introducing us. We squatted at the foot of the berimbaus. I remember looking up at all the great mestres as the music started. Then Cravo and I played, and it was probably the worst game I had played in years. I was nervous and rushed. Luckily we soon moved on, each of us playing five or six mestres, which was a great honor in itself. And that was it—we were given our new cords and sent on our way.

*Mestres Suassuna, Bandeira, Rã, Acordeon, Berkeley, 2000.*

*Cravo and me at our graduation, Berkeley, 2000.*

*With Mestre Rã, Berkeley, 2000.*

After the formatura, Marta and I prepared for our move to Sacramento. Marta was willing but ambivalent about leaving the Bay Area. She left the final decision to me. It was not too late to change course—we could stay in the Bay Area. Marta had already made a few friends there. I had friends there too, and the door was still open for me to keep my position at Head Over Heels. We would be secure and in a familiar environment. But the Bay Area was already saturated with top-notch capoeira and Brazilian dance teachers. We would never be able to realize our dreams there, not to the scale we were bent on.

Moving to Sacramento and building careers in capoeira and dance would be a leap into the unknown. We'd be starting over with next to nothing and no safety net. I was afraid but determined. We were on a quest to make our dreams come true. For me, this was a turning point, like that one in Israel all those years before. A fork in the road. One way: comfort, routine, safety. The other way: challenge, newness, danger. The second way was scary, but it was the road to something extraordinary. I didn't want to live beholden to my fears, and to never know if we could have made it. I told Marta my thoughts, and she agreed.

My buddy Peik had kindly given me his old Audi sedan. Marta and I packed our few belongings and set out to Sacramento on a weekday in mid-August. This was it—a grand adventure and a new phase in both our lives. No matter what happened, nothing would ever be the same for either of us.

As soon as we arrived in Sacramento, Marta and I devoted ourselves to starting our dance and capoeira programs. We set up a preliminary, one-time set of workshops to develop interest and launch our ongoing classes. A dance studio in central Sacramento called Step 1 rented us space on Saturdays for our initial workshops and ongoing classes. I reserved the space a month in advance, and during that month we promoted the workshops every way and everywhere we could. We put up flyers all over town. I asked dance studios, cultural centers, and martial arts schools to help promote us. Marta and I dropped in at dance classes, sometimes unannounced, and introduced ourselves. We visited Dr. Linda Goodrich's Afro-Caribbean dance class at California State University, Sacramento. This honored matriarch of the local ethnic dance scene gave us a warm welcome and let us promote our classes to her students. In coming years, Dr. Goodrich would be a valuable ally.

I called the people we knew of who were interested in capoeira in Sacramento, including Magen and Dom. Another man, Scott, had learned capoeira from Mestre Amen in Los Angeles and had given Mestre Acordeon his phone number. I offered these three an informal class prior to the workshops, and they accepted. We met one evening in

McKinley Park, and Dom brought along his friend Doc. There on the grassy lawn, I taught a brief class and we had a little roda.

The day of the workshops came and we nervously headed to Step 1. We had no idea how many people would be there—maybe dozens, maybe none. I would have been happy to have at least ten people in each workshop. The schedule included an hour-and-a-half capoeira workshop immediately followed by Marta's samba workshop of the same length. We had our music CDs in order, and I had my berimbau, atabaque, and pandeiro. I had called some people in Berkeley and asked them to help—Bateria and Leitão were on their way.

We arrived twenty minutes before class. A small crowd of people was milling around in the Step 1 lobby area. I asked the front desk attendant what they were there for, and she said it was my class. Surprised, I invited them into the studio. There were already more than ten people, and more streamed in as I chatted and arranged my instruments and CDs. By class time, there were more than thirty people.

Bateria and Leitão helped me start the class with a brief demonstration. Next I led a warm-up and taught ginga and a few fundamentals. The students were a diverse mix of dancers, martial artists, and other athletic types, including men and women of various ethnicities. My four original students from the park were there, and Marta joined us. Over the next year or so, she and I consistently participated in each other's classes, if only to help fill them out. At the end of the session we had a roda. Bateria organized and led the music. Everyone got a chance to play, and I tried to impress by doing some acrobatics. Afterwards I thanked everyone and handed out flyers for my ongoing classes starting the next week.

Marta took over to teach her samba workshop. Her class was full as well. She introduced herself and explained her background in Portuguese, which I translated. She led a warm-up of slow movements to the rhythm of afoxé, slow African Brazilian music that Bateria and I played live. Next she played CDs from Bahia, and her class progressed into samba and axé. At the end she had all the students form a circle and take turns entering it solo or in pairs. She warmly thanked all the students and distributed flyers for her ongoing classes also starting the next week.

We headed home elated. The workshops had been a big success. More than sixty people had come to one or both of our workshops! *Wow*, I thought. If it's going to be like this, we'd have no problem launching our programs. We both knew it wouldn't be that easy, but the great turnout was encouraging, and we were optimistic.

In addition to our Saturdays at Step 1, I rented space on Monday and Wednesday evenings at the Washington Neighborhood Center. This modest old community center near downtown Sacramento was built in the 1950s to serve underprivileged youths. It was known for its boxing program, which was still active at the time. Unfortunately the center had received little funding in recent decades and was rundown. It had some great wall murals but was dilapidated, worn, and dirty. The small basketball court we used had a concrete floor and was freezing cold in the winter. When it rained, the roof leaked prodigiously. But they let me pay a percentage of whatever money I made from my classes, which would be nearly nothing to start, and they had convenient evening times available. Marta's classes were at Step 1 on Saturdays and at a small belly-dance studio on Tuesday and Thursday evenings.

Eager for my first Monday class, I showed up early at the Washington Center. I spent an hour mopping the floor and otherwise making the place as presentable as possible. The original four students from our class in the park arrived, as did Marta and two guys from the workshop, Mario and

Steven. Not a big group, but big enough. I enthusiastically led them through class, including some basics, a few acrobatics, and a roda.

The next evening I took Marta to her samba class. She also had about half a dozen students. I played some of the music and translated for her. On Wednesday we were back at the Washington Center for capoeira. Thursday was Marta's class. On Saturday we both taught at Step 1. We were also staying busy with other work. I taught gymnastics at Beyer's, and Marta cleaned houses most weekdays. We kept up this schedule for the next year or so, working hard and struggling financially. Classes were usually small, but this was what we had signed up for.

When I wasn't working or teaching, I promoted our classes all over town. I spent hours posting flyers on lampposts and cars and in cafés and laundromats. Many times I took my berimbau and a stack of flyers to a park, square, or college campus. I would play berimbau and do my own capoeira workout to demonstrate. Most people hurried by, but if any curious soul approached, I explained what I was doing, offered a flyer, and encouraged him or her to come try a class. I went to the public library and checked out Jay Levinson's book on guerrilla marketing. I think it was there I found the idea of placing my flyers in books about capoeira and other martial arts in bookstores and libraries.

My efforts produced few results. The return was tiny in proportion to all the energy I was spending. It was tempting to see it as a waste of time, but I knew it would take a sustained effort to build a capoeira program and career. Not only was I starting from scratch, but there was almost no existing market for capoeira. Hardly anyone even knew what it was. A career path was not established—few people had taught capoeira in the U.S. at that point, and none of them were non-Brazilian. I was helping construct a new occupation while introducing an unknown art form to the Sacramento community. It wasn't like becoming a doctor, lawyer, cook, or carpenter. It wasn't even like becoming a teacher of mainstream martial arts.

To think success would come after anything less than persistent effort over years would be unrealistic. So I kept at it, hoping my efforts would pay off eventually. Occasionally I had a class with only one or two students, but I swallowed my disappointment, forced a smile, and gave the best class I could. When once or twice I had a class for which nobody showed up, I nursed a broken heart on my way home and resolved to work even harder. When now and then the class was big or a new student signed up, I rejoiced and pumped an inner fist, continuing my work with renewed enthusiasm.

The income from cleaning houses, teaching gymnastics, and our capoeira and samba classes wasn't enough to sustain Marta and me, so I took a job as a waiter at a local restaurant. This was a bitter pill to swallow. It had been several years since I had worked in restaurants, and it felt like a big step backward. It was not what I had hoped to be doing as I entered my thirties. Restaurant work is honest work, but at this point in my life, burning plates, demanding customers, yelling cooks and managers, and the rest of it, felt degrading. The humiliation was worse if one of my capoeira students ate there. I felt deflated and embarrassed to be seen in an apron taking orders. I wanted them to think of me as their dynamic capoeira teacher, not a waiter at a pizza joint. But I swallowed my pride, and hoped for a time when my work with capoeira would support me.

Through the winter of 2000 to 2001, capoeira classes were small, a handful of us training in the freezing Washington Community Center gym and at Step 1 on Saturdays. But things picked up that spring. Guerrilla marketing was finally paying off, and new students were finding my classes. Many came and went, but a few stayed and became excellent students and fine capoeiristas.

Now that I was a capoeira teacher, it was part of my job to assign my students Portuguese nicknames, called apelidos. Capoeira apelidos are seldom politically correct or complimentary. More often they are humorous, teasing references to some aspect of character or appearance. Someone with big upper front teeth might be called Coelho, Rabbit. If one's face turns red, Lagosta, Lobster, or if someone is big and tall Montanha, Mountain. Mestre Acordeon's name means accordion, the instrument he has played since childhood. He often spoke about capoeira nicknames and their difference from American nicknames. He mentioned a U.S. student who wanted the nickname Lion Heart and said no Brazilian would give such a grandiose name.

Marta's Portuguese and cultural understanding helped a lot in giving apelidos. With her help we named Dom Tigre, meaning Tiger, for his eager attitude and powerful athleticism. Doc was Relampago, Lightning, for his speed but also because he crashed into things sometimes. Robert was Sabiá, Songbird, because he liked to sing and had a good voice. Babyfaced Steven became Moleque, Street Urchin. Scott we named Professore because he was a teacher, and Jon was Palito, Toothpick, for his stiff posture. Magen received the name Caxias, meaning a studious, hardworking pupil. Joel became Irmão, Brother, because he called everyone "bro" and became like a brother to many of us.

Most of these students stayed a long time and became the core of our group. Irmão, Caxias, and Sabiá eventually graduated and are still active in capoeira to this day. Relampago is still active, and Moleque came and went for years. Professore and Palito trained hard and consistently for eight or nine years. Tigre stopped after a couple of years, but a decade later placed his daughter in my classes. Later came

Bode, Macarrão, Tornado, Castanho, Bebida, Ursinho, Força, Leopoldão, and Borbulias who went on to be one of my first graduates. There was also Sonho, Lagartixa, Caçador, Imperador, Vampiro, Travessa, and more. These students were a part of the creation and development of our group, and my career. They believed in me as a capoeira teacher, and for this I am forever grateful.

I moved my classes to East Wind Martial Arts studio, a modest upgrade from the Washington Center. Although it was dry and had some degree of temperature control, it was poorly maintained and in a less desirable neighborhood. Nevertheless I was slowly acquiring more students. I had my first class with more than twenty students, an event I celebrated and will always remember. I also hosted Mestre Rã and Mestre Acordeon to teach their first Sacramento workshops, introducing them with great pride.

It was around this time we had our first television news exposure. As part of my ongoing marketing campaign I had sent press releases to all the major media outlets. Channel 31's *Good Day Sacramento* picked us up and sent a camera crew and TV personality to do a segment on us. It was early in the morning, but Marta and I rallied a bunch of our students and demonstrated capoeira and samba on live television. Over the following years, we would make many such TV appearances.

The year 2000, so significant and eventful in our lives, was drawing to a close. So much had happened: Brazil, meeting Marta, her arrival in the U.S., graduation, moving to Sacramento, and starting a new life. It was an undeniably pivotal year. But it wasn't over yet. One more big event was still to come.

Marta's six-month tourist visa had almost expired, and she didn't want to stay illegally, so she gave me an ultimatum. Either we would marry so she could be a legal resident, or she would go back to Brazil. I considered my options. We had gotten off to a fairly good start in Sacramento. It was a struggle to get by, and our classes were still quite small, but we had known this was going to be the case and had made good progress. We still didn't really know each other well. We had good times, but we also fought. We had worked hard and already achieved some goals. We couldn't break up now and go our separate ways.

After a few days of hand-wringing, I agreed to marry Marta. On a cold December morning at the Sacramento County Clerk's office, we exchanged rings and vows and received a marriage certificate. I was now a married man.

# CHAPTER FOURTEEN

# Opening an Academy

We had been in Sacramento for almost a year and decided to hold our first batizado. Calling Mestre Acordeon and Mestre Rã, I got their approval and scheduled a date that they could be there. I invited a couple of other teachers as well, including Mestre Urubu, Professor Galo, and Professor Dondi. Then I dove into the work of organizing the event, including drafting a budget, renting a hall from the city recreation department, designing a flyer, ordering t-shirts, promoting the event, and recruiting volunteers.

Just before the batizado, I leased a commercial space to make into our own studio. We got the keys one week before the batizado and hosted a housewarming maculelê workshop and roda with our students and a few guests the night before the event.

The day of our batizado, Sacramento's first, I was a nervous. As the students, mestres, and other guests arrived at the hall I paced worriedly outside. Participants and spectators filled the hall. I did my best to follow the outline and etiquette my mestres had demonstrated at many batizados before. My students did a maculelê performance, and Marta's students performed samba and afoxé choreographies. Twenty-three of my students played the assembled teachers and earned their first cords.

*Our first batizado with Professore, Caxias, me, Relampago, and Tigre, Sacramento, 2001.*

Immediately after the batizado, we went to work building out our new studio. I borrowed a few thousand dollars and spent it on a wood floor, mirrors, paint, and furniture. Soon we had a modest but authentic capoeira and samba academy ready to go, and opened our doors. We called it the Brazilian Arts Center.

That December, 2001, Marta and I traveled to Brazil for a wedding ceremony there. It was largely for her family but some of mine made it too, including my father, my sister Mora, my cousin Marisa and her husband, and my nephew Ryan. My students Caxias and Krishna also came. We spent the whole trip in Bahia, which was warm and sunny, as it was summer there. At the wedding, Mestre Pescoso, who taught in Humboldt, California, showed up along with some of his students and the legendary Mestre Leopoldina. This colorful character was of Rio de Janeiro capoeira's old guard. He didn't know anyone in the wedding but enthusiastically threw rice at us when we walked down the aisle. Later, we traveled to Marta's family's hometown, a small village in the delta. On Christmas Day, we played capoeira with the local group on a white sand beach.

*My father and mother visited our first batizado.*

Back in Sacramento, I got to work promoting our classes and developing my capoeira program. This was the formative period of the capoeira group I was founding, and I cultivated its identity with care. I drew a school logo, a circular pointillism design based on a photo of me and one of my Berkeley friends. I waited to name our group, thinking it best to let its identity reveal itself. For the time being, we simply went by United Capoeira Association—Sacramento.

Our pedigree was already determined and fortunately excellent.

I chose a group-centric approach, emphasizing the students. The group identity would be as much about them as me. Some teachers emphasized their celebrity appeal and attracted students with that. I enjoyed organizing, teaching, and directing but didn't want to be a star. In fact, I've been shy and socially awkward my whole life. The more I could deflect the limelight, the better. Plus I felt this strategy might yield better long-term student retention, as they might feel like important parts of the community, not just loyal followers.

*Cover photo. Me with another Capoeira Brazil group, Bahia, 2001.*

One of my goals was to create and maintain a truly egalitarian space. From those earliest days, I cultivated a neutral atmosphere in regard to gender, race, sexual orientation, and age. I always strove to give everyone equal treatment, and insisted on the same from everyone who came through our doors.

*One of my first kids classes, Sacramento, 2001.*

Our business was small, independent, and strictly local. We never allowed any corporate influence in our group or the business. It was my view that big business existed for the sole purpose of making money, a philosophy I despised. It was my impression that corporations were responsible for poisoning the environment, corrupting the political system, and widespread social injustice. Our business didn't exist primarily for capital gain. Its reasons were higher. We had to make a living, but the values of community, integrity, health, and artistic expression were more important than material wealth. There would be no Coca-Cola signs or Nike swooshes in our academy.

I waited several years before giving our capoeira group a name of its own besides U.C.A.—Sacramento. My students' enthusiasm and unquenchable thirst impressed me and reminded me of myself back in the Berkeley days. They also reminded me of the phrase água de beber, the metaphor for thirst for knowledge. Also, Sacramento is known as the "River City," água de beber has a poetic ring, and I hadn't heard of another group with that name. It was perfect. From then on we called ourselves Capoeira Água de Beber, or just ADB for short.

*Mestre Acordeon visits Sacramento, 2003.*

By mid-2002 my teaching career was beginning to take off. I was making little money but was plenty busy running around all over town to teach and do demos. I taught adult capoeira classes at the studio Monday, Wednesday, and Friday nights, and Saturdays at noon. We did not yet have children's classes at the studio, but I taught kids in various after-school programs and through the city Parks and Recreation program. Altogether I taught about 500 classes that year, a pace I would maintain for two decades. The group was slowly growing, and we acquired several more talented, dedicated students.

The studio just managed to pay for itself, so Marta and I continued to work additional jobs. I continued working unhappily at the restaurant for a while, but then was hired as a middle school physical education teacher. Thrilled to have a full-time job with good pay, I dove into the work. Once classes began, however, my outlook changed. The P.E. classes had more than forty children in each class period, five periods per day. The school was in a socioeconomically challenged area, and many of the kids came from families with severe financial and emotional problems. Worst of all, I was significantly undertrained and unprepared.

The first several weeks, I battled desperately against the kids' wills and my own lack of skills and organization to get lessons and activities going. I even tried to teach them some capoeira, perhaps with a romantic notion of turning around kids' lives like in the movie *Only the Strong*. But by the second month, I felt so exhausted and defeated I was just letting the kids have free time on the blacktop each period.

To promote our classes our students and Marta and I did demonstrations and performances at schools, festivals, parties, or anywhere else they would have us. Our first shows were short and simple, since our students barely knew anything yet. Marta and her students would dance while my students and I pounded a rhythm on our batucada drums. Then we would put together a spirited if rudimentary roda. Marta played pandeiro and I berimbau. We performed every chance we could, even traveling a little bit. When we performed together with my old friend Mestre Amunka and his group in the Cinco de Mayo parade in Calistoga, California, together we won first place in the band category.

In June I received a call from Dr. Goodrich, who had welcomed us into the local arts scene a couple years before. She said the California State Fair was going to put on a large Carnaval production. Each night of the fair, the Brazilianthemed Bay Area group Fogo na Roupa would give a live show, then lead a parade through the fairgrounds. Would we like to be the opening act for each of these performances? Marta and I needed little discussion before saying yes.

*ADB at Whole Earth Festival, Davis, California, 2003.*

The State Fair is every August at the Cal Expo convention and fairgrounds complex in Sacramento. We attended a few nights of rehearsals there, and then opening night arrived. Backstage, we warmed up and reviewed our routines. Our show opened with an afoxé dance set. Then we performed a capoeira demonstration, some maculelê, and a batucada and samba finale. Fogo na Roupa assembled on stage behind us, and as we struck our last note, they launched into their set with thunderous percussion.

Their show was about an hour long and included various genres of Brazilian music. One of their songs contained berimbau, so a couple of our capoeiristas jumped on stage and performed a little capoeira. After Fogo's set, we joined them for the parade through the fairgrounds. Our combined percussion groups, along with an eclectic assortment of stilt walkers, samba dancers, the California Bear, and other performers, marched and played music from one end of Cal Expo to the other. When we left the fair that night, we were exhilarated and exhausted.

*Tornado and me with Saco de Osso, Esqueleto, Macarrão, Bode, and Relampago, Sacramento, 2003.*

We repeated this performance every night for twenty-two nights straight. Under pressure to rise to the occasion, all our skills increased dramatically. We learned a lot from Fogo na Roupa and their director, Carlos Aceituno. In addition to being bandleader, Carlos was a capoeira mestre, as well as a kind and generous man. He joined our capoeira demonstration several times, gave us tips on performing, and allowed us to play with Fogo na Roupa, from whom we picked up new music skills.

That September, we held our second annual batizado. We rented a theater at the Sierra 2 community center and preceded the ceremony with a musical and theatrical production. Marta and I directed it, a medley of Brazilian dances and music and several short skits. We called it "A Day in Bahia." It was meant to capture that magical city's ambiance and culture. It included elaborate choreographies and parts for each of our students, and it lasted way too long: nearly three hours. When it was finally time to start the batizado, the hour was late, and I suspect many of the participants would have liked to go to bed. Our guest teachers included Mestre Acordeon, Mestre Rã, Mestre Urubu, Professor Samuka, and the famous Mestre Nestor Capoeira, author of the well-known *The Little Capoeira Book*.

The next spring, I happily ended my brief career as a public school teacher. From this point on I only worked with capoeira. Through the small income now coming from the studio, outside teaching gigs, and the occasional performance, we squeezed out a meager living. We were poor, but happy to be doing what we loved. Without other jobs straining my time and energy, I resumed my marketing campaign. This, along with the momentum gained from almost three years of sustained efforts, brought a surge in enrollment. I now had about forty capoeira students at the studio, plus some taking my classes in nearby Davis and other locations.

My capoeira group was doing great, but I was out of shape. I had numerous physical problems, including plantar fasciitis, plantar warts, and back and knee injuries. I also felt spent from marketing and teaching, my metabolism had slowed, and I was eating a lot of Marta's rich Brazilian food. For the first time in my adult life I had gained weight, and my belly and face had a puffiness I had never seen before. I couldn't do some of the moves I had done at my formatura. Part of the problem was that I had lost my joy in capoeira. Physical pain, along with the stress of building a group and opening an academy, had taken the fun out of capoeira.

After years of pain and treatment, most of my bodily ailments eventually healed and passed. Gathering myself for another push, I planned out a new regimen. Limiting my diet, I ran, lifted weights, and met students at to practice acrobatics every week. Soon I had shed the excess pounds, and before long I regained my previous skills plus some.

*Macarrão and I, Sutter's Fort, Sacramento, 2004.*

In my first several years in Sacramento, I seldom left the area in order to maintain consistency in the capoeira program I was building. Now it was somewhat established and I started to travel more. Playing in different rodas with other advanced people again revealed something: my understanding of the game and my eye for strategy had improved through the process of teaching. The challenge then was for my body to keep up. But I was starting to get back in good shape, and maybe more importantly, enjoying the game again.

*Maculelê in our first academy, Sacramento, 2003.*

Eventually I did get back into peak shape and entered one of the heights of my athletic career. I was fast and strong, could do some respectable acrobatics, and my perception was sharp. A decade before, I had wanted to be "great" at capoeira, to have an exciting game like the top capoeiristas. Maybe this was never the case, but if it was, it was probably during this time.

Contrary to the positive direction of my capoeira game and career, my relationship with Marta was falling apart. Ours was a conflict of personalities and cultures, and neither of us was well equipped to deal with it. We had devolved into a never-ending cycle of arguments and insecurity. I tried everything I could think of, including love, reassurance, and seeing a bilingual couple's therapist. But instead of improving, problems worsened. Finally, after months of deliberation and consultation with trusted friends and family, I decided to separate from Marta. We moved out of the apartment we were in and into separate homes.

The breakup was painful and sad, but Marta remained mostly calm. I wondered if this was because she thought we might reunite. Whatever the reason, I was grateful. We awkwardly continued to work together at the studio and sorted out our respective situations. For a time this worked, us coexisting as friends and business associates. Then Marta had a big meltdown and there were several horrible, public scenes. That was the end of our relationship for me, and I filed for divorce.

In late 2004 we closed the Brazilian Arts Center, severing the last tie between Marta and I. She continued teaching her classes at a local community center, and I opened a new studio on Sacramento's north side. It was tempting to view our relationship as a mistake. But despite all the drama and pain, together we had created something bigger than either of us could have alone. The work we had done teaching, performing, and building community, was special. It had enriched people's lives, enhanced the city we lived in, and launched both of us into our respective careers.

# CHAPTER FIFTEEN

# Under Siege

*B*waap bwaap bwaap bwaap! The alarm woke me abruptly. I jumped out of bed, scared. *What's going on? What time is it?* 3:15 a.m. Why was the alarm sounding in the middle of the night? *Someone's breaking into the studio again!*

About a year before this, I had rented a property that included commercial space for the academy and a house in back where I lived. It was on Del Paso Boulevard on Sacramento's north side, a once lively area now derelict and depressed. Aside from the location, the property was a young martial arts instructor's dream. The studio had big windows facing the boulevard and a rollup door in back that opened to a large courtyard with an avocado tree. The house had a large garage downstairs and a two-bedroom apartment upstairs.

A stone wall with big metal gates surrounded the compound, which was good since the neighborhood was rough. In the first six months we experienced two break-ins into the studio. Bracing for more and determined to defend our home and academy, I bought a baseball bat and had an alarm system installed. I also adopted a shelter dog, a rottweiler and German sheppard mix. She was a big, beautiful one-year-old, with mostly black hair and a somber demeanor. I named her Sombra, which means "shadow," in Portuguese.

I grabbed the baseball bat and called for Sombra. The police should be on their way, but I wasn't waiting for them. Barefoot and wearing only shorts, I entered the courtyard. My heart pounded as we approached the studio's back door.

The alarm was still blaring, but I tried to unlock the door quietly anyway. I opened it and peeked inside. There was no one just inside the door. I stepped in carefully with Sombra, bat raised and ready for somebody to come at me. A light was on in the office, and I could see a big hole in the front door, and broken glass on the floor. *There's somebody inside here right now!*

Listening and scanning every corner, I made my way step by step onto the large floor. As I reached the center of the studio, I could see inside the office. There, behind my desk, a man was sitting in the chair and going through the drawers.

Just as I saw him, the man looked up and saw me. For a long moment we both froze, staring at each other. He seemed unhurried, not rushed despite the blaring alarm and my arrival. I thought frantically about if he had a gun, but remained still. Then Sombra walked into the office and approached the man. He tensed but remained still also. She sniffed him a couple of times, then meandered back out of the office. Glancing at me, she headed for the back door.

"Sombra!" I called urgently.

She gave me another furtive glance, then continued out of the studio.

"Sombra!" I yelled, but she was gone.

The man was still just staring at me. *Why is he still here?* The alarm had been going off for several minutes now, the police were presumably on their way, and I was standing there with a baseball bat. He should have been long gone. *Did he have a gun?*

Not knowing what else to do, I stepped forward and began screaming at him. "Motherfucker! Get the hell out of here! I'm gonna fuck you up, you piece of shit!"

Finally, he jumped up and came running out of the office. I dropped into a low stance and readied the bat. There was no need, though. He turned to the front door and quickly dove through the hole in the glass. In a flash he was away down the street.

Shaken, I looked around. The police should have been there. I wanted them to see everything as it was, so I didn't clean or move anything. I sat cross-legged in the middle of the floor, my bat on my lap, and waited. A half-hour passed, and still the police had not shown up. I went into the office and called them. It turned out the alarm system had malfunctioned and failed to alert them.

The police finally arrived, and I left them in the studio for a moment while I got dressed. I spent the rest of the night reporting to the police, cleaning up glass, and guarding the studio. In the morning, I called the glass installer for yet another door repair. Eventually, when things were calm, Sombra came back down to the studio.

During the first winter in this space, I remodeled and built out the new academy. As before, my students supplied a lot of help. The business was a sole proprietorship, now under my name only. Although the capoeira group was doing well, the business barely broke even. Without the samba program, and now in a bigger space, it was a struggle to stay afloat. We could only have so many capoeira classes a week, and it was difficult to fill the studio the rest of the time. I had planned to rent it to other teachers or dance groups, but few materialized.

All of this served to reveal my lack of business skills. For my main source of income, capoeira tuition, I simply accepted students' tuition by hand in the form of check or cash each month. Often dependent on the whims of circumstance for consistency of payment, this method is terrible not only for income but also for student-teacher relationships. Meanwhile, besides some guerrilla marketing, I knew nothing about public relations, client management, or online advertising. It would still be a few years until a better way emerged. In the meantime I struggled along, living hand-to-mouth with no savings or benefits. Every time tuition dried up was a financial crisis, and I scrambled to make ends meet.

Not long after moving into the neighborhood, its challenges became apparent. By day, Del Paso Boulevard was mostly deserted with almost no foot traffic. At night, gunshots rang nearby, groups of teens swarmed and got into fights, and there were always one or two prostitutes working on our block. The hole-in-the-wall bar across the street was a center for methamphetamine use. One night, one of the patrons walked out of the bar and into a street fight. He was knocked down, hit his head on a curb, and died. Another night, my roommate Garrett woke me and led me to the kitchen window. In the courtyard below was a SWAT commando team, complete with assault rifles and body armor, fanning out inside the property from the back gate. Seeing us above, they demanded to know if we were the residents. We assured them we were.

One evening I noticed a man hanging out in front of the studio. He was middle-aged, had a shopping cart full of stuff, and looked drunk. None of this was unusual, but a couple of the female students arriving at the studio for beginner's class said he had made inappropriate remarks to them. I stepped out and politely asked him to respect our patrons. At the end of class an hour later, the man was still there and speaking to passersby. I went out and explained that this was my business, and would he please move. Slurring his words slightly, he assured me he would leave.

A few minutes later, he was still here. This time I raised my voice and told him to leave immediately. He ignored me.

"Hey!" I said.

He moved toward the front door, and I sidestepped to block him. He looked intently at me, then went to his shopping cart a few yards away. He pulled out two window squeegees, the metal and rubber wipers you find at gas stations, and started slicing and swinging them like nunchuks. He was good and did a whole nunchuck routine, advancing toward me. He didn't look drunk anymore, but rather like a skilled martial artist. I stood my ground, blocking the front door. All my students had gathered inside the window, watching. A couple of guys stepped outside behind me.

The man came at me, squeegees swinging. I sprang forward with a benção, a straight kick, to his chest, knocking him backward. He regained his balance, and we both stood still for a moment, eyeing each other. Suddenly he put away his squeegees and pushed his cart away down the street. One more situation resolved.

In 2005 I attended the annual batizado in Berkeley as I did every year. My mestres' school had grown, and the event was huge. It lasted five days and drew hundreds of capoeiristas from around the world, including many of the top mestres. These included Mestre Gato, Mestre Suassuna, Mestre Urubu, and Mestre Amen. Mestre Joel, a well-known teacher from São Paulo whom we had visited several times, was there. Mestre Barrão, Capoeira Axé's founder, and Mestre Bimba's student Mestre Deputado attended. Mestre Suassuna's student Mestre Canguru came, and others.

For us longtime United Capoeira Association members, these events were like family reunions. Most U.C.A. students and teachers were there, plus many other friends. These included Pedro Cruz and Mariano, two young Brazilian teachers who had started teaching around the same time I had. Pedro taught in Portland, Oregon, and Mariano in Santa Barbara. Both had done great work building capoeira groups in their respective cities.

*Cigano, me, and Dondi become Contramestres, Berkeley, 2005.*

I think it was Mariano who tipped me off that something special was in the works that year. He said he had overheard something, and I had a surprise coming my way. He wouldn't say more, and I didn't think much of it. A couple days later, though, Mestre Acordeon and Mestre Rã summoned me to their office, as they had five years before. This time they informed me I would be promoted to the level of contramestre at the batizado. Surprised and happy, I thanked them for the honor. I received the new title and cord along with Dondi and a teacher from Mexico named Cigano. My new title was Contramestre Galego, which my students shortened to CMG.

*United Capoeira Association formatura, Berkeley, 2005.*

A few months later in Sacramento, two dogs attacked Sombra. We were taking a walk when she stopped to sniff at a fence. In a flash, a large pit bull appeared, lunging at her through the bars of the fence and biting down on her snout. Sombra let out a horrible squeal and tried to pull back, but the pit had bit in hard. Its head was squeezed between the fence bars. Behind it, another large pit bull was furiously trying to reach us.

Sombra tried to pull away, and I tried to help, but it was no use—the pit bit down harder. Blood dripped from Sombra's face, and she cried piteously. I pulled harder but was afraid of hurting her more. Her pulls started to weaken. I kept pulling and looked around. I yelled to some neighbors for help, and they ignored me. Desperate, I moved to Sombra's side. The pit bull's face protruded through the fence. While still pulling Sombra's leash with one arm, I kicked the pit's face hard, near its jaws. It just looked at me, not loosening its grip on poor Sombra.

Panicky now, I kicked the dog's head again and again as hard as I could, more than twenty times. The whole side of its face was bludgeoned, but still it did not let go. It was starting to win the battle, dragging Sombra deeper between the fence bars, where the other dog was raging. I yelled at the neighbors again, begging for help. Finally a landscaper came over with a bottle of pesticide. He sprayed pesticide into the pit's nose and eyes as I kicked. Finally the pit let go, its face bloody and eyes swollen. Sombra and I tumbled backward. She fell on top of me as I fell onto the sidewalk. Blood was everywhere.

*Portland, Oregon, 2005.*

Shakily thanking the man for his help, I picked up my dog and carried her across the street. There, some kindly shopkeepers helped us get cleaned up. Within a week

Sombra was fine—except that for the rest of her life, she would have a scar across her nose.

Despite all the unfortunate incidences, this was a good time in some ways. Around North America there was a lot of new interest and enthusiasm for capoeira. Groups like the one I founded, Galo's in Colorado, Dondi's in Tucson, along with many others, grew in size and skill level. Each year we tried to outdo each other with bigger and better batizados, higher performing students, and more involvement in each other's events. New groups were springing up left and right. In Sacramento, in addition to our capoeira program, we put on a lot of fun and successful events including live music and other performances.

*From left, Txell, Budhina, Bode, me, Tornado, Castanho, Faceira,*
*Sacramento State University, 2006.*

Nevertheless, behind the scenes, I was struggling. Two years under siege from the area's nefarious forces culminated in the 3:00 a.m. break-in. Then there was the stress of chronic financial near-ruin. I was constantly on edge and nervous. I slept little, waking at every noise. Thankfully, there wasn't another break-in, but there were other events involving addicts, robberies, prostitutes, johns, and the like. I wanted to move out, but I was only halfway through a five-year lease, and had nowhere else to go anyway.

It was depressing and felt unsustainable. Things were bad, and I couldn't see a light at the end of the tunnel. This was the one time I seriously considered giving up. Perhaps I had been wrong all along. Maybe this whole having a unique career and running a capoeira academy idea was nonsense. I thought about closing shop and taking some normal job. Or perhaps doing something irresponsible like dropping everything to bum around Mexico for as long as I could. But instead I just continued to teach, and defend the compound, and assured everyone that everything was good.

## CHAPTER SIXTEEN

# Return to Royal Gorge

Wind whistled through the scrubby cedar trees clinging to the rocky cliffs. Below us, the earth dropped away into Royal Gorge. Across the Gorge and upstream was the steep terrain where I had tracked the bear and her cub almost twenty years before. Between that place and where I stood, a hawk soared, a thousand feet in the air but level with my eye. It was an amazing view. Too bad the situation wasn't better. I shifted my position, and my hiking boot sent a few small rocks tumbling down the steep hill.

My dog and I were nestled behind a wiry dwarf tree that was preventing us from also tumbling down the vertical terrain. Sombra's head lay heavily in my lap. She still couldn't sit up, but at least her breathing was regular now. Poor dog. And it was my fault. I had bitten off more than she could chew. Now at the tail end of a three-day backpacking trip in the Sierras, her life was in danger, and we were stranded on a mountainside in the wilderness. Unable to climb up or down, we waited for Pinga and Irmão to rescue us.

Pingo and Irmão were my longtime friends, students, and fellow adventurers. They had accompanied me and Sombra on this trip to Royal Gorge, site of my long ago "vision quest." I had hoped a return to nature and the home of my early inspiration might cure what ailed me now. We had loaded up my Jeep with our packs and driven into the Sierra Mountains, stopping briefly at the Cedars to say hello to my old boss Jim. It had been a challenge to find the trailhead way out on Wabena Ridge in a maze of four-wheel-drive roads. This trail wasn't listed in any guidebooks, and time had obscured my memory.

*Royal Gorge and Snow Mountain from Wabena Ridge.*

Once we reached the place, we peered over the crest into the gorge below. In this my memory had been true—it was grand. Spectacularly steep walls plummeted into the forested chasm, the river, a blue and white ribbon, wound its way at the bottom. Eager to explore and reach the falls, we hoisted our packs. Sombra had her own saddlebags carrying dog food and a blanket. The going was easy as we began our descent into the massive canyon, and we enjoyed being out in the wild and breathing fresh, pine-scented air.

About two-thirds of the way down, we rounded a bend and were surprised to see the trail ahead of us give way to a gulf of empty space. Creeping up to the edge where the earth dropped off, we saw that a massive landslide had taken out the trail and left a deep ravine in its place. The ravine's sides were crumbling cliffs about thirty feet deep. Someone had secured ropes to trees on either side of the ravine for rappelling and climbing in and out. Treacherous at best for us humans, there was no way Sombra could do this. Perplexed, we sat down to rest and ponder our options.

We decided Irmão and Pinga would lower themselves down the cliff, and I would lower our packs to them. Then I would take Sombra uphill in search of another way that was more accessible for her. We completed the first phase of the operation while Sombra whined and fretted. Then she and I set out uphill through the forest, following the edge of the ravine. After a short distance we found an area. It was still difficult to navigate, with crumbling and shifting rock, but it was gradual enough for a dog to traverse. We made our way down and met with Pinga and Irmão. They had found a spring of fresh water gushing straight from the rock. We all refreshed ourselves with the pure, cold spring water.

The ravine's other wall was not quite as steep. We managed to get Sombra up the cliff by tying a rope around her. While one of us pushed her up from below, another pulled from above. Then we continued on our way down the trail, beneath towering conifers. We arrived at the gorge's bottom and found Rattlesnake Falls. Irmão and Pinga agreed that I had not exaggerated its beauty and grandeur. We spent all of that day and the next swimming, exploring, and jumping off cliffs into the crystal clear water. It felt so good to be there, playing on the rocks and river, immersed in the elements. I remembered my mushroom-fueled epiphany so many years before, when I saw connections amongst everything.

After two nights, it was time to go. We set out on the trail relaxed and happy, but I worried about getting Sombra across the ravine. When we reached it, we assessed our options. Looking down over the drop-off's edge, I realized it would be more difficult to take her down than it had been to bring her up. And once in the ravine, coming out of it on the other side would be dangerous as well. Plus, her paws were already raw from the first crossing. It was then I had a bad idea—to head straight uphill, off the trail, to search for a way around the whole landslide area. Irmão and Pinga attempted to dissuade me but eventually agreed to follow my lead.

We spent the rest of the afternoon clawing our way through difficult terrain and never again found the top of the ravine or the trail. Shortly after leaving the trail, we encountered a steep section that was almost a cliff. After struggling over it, almost falling several times, it was clear it would be impossible to go back down. Now we were committed to this route and had to find a way to the ridge top. After we had spent several hours pushing through thick bushes and climbing steep rocks, Sombra showed signs of fatigue. We all did, but for a dog it was harder to get past all the obstacles. And our water supply was running low.

We rested in a manzanita thicket. I heard a distinct buzzing sound. Irmão, who was ten or twenty yards ahead of us, looked back and froze. "Galego!" he shouted. "Run! You're standing on a beehive!"

I looked down. Buzzing around our feet was a swarm of bees. Just then I felt the first sting on my ankle, and as I rushed to grab my dog, another on my hand. Hoisting Sombra by her collar, I pounded through the bushes, leaping over some and stepping on others. Not stopping until we were well away, the dog and I slumped on the ground. My stings were only an annoyance, but Sombra's face was swelling up. We didn't know exactly where we were, but it was undoubtedly still a long way from the ridge top and our vehicle.

"Guys," I said. "What are we going to do? I don't know if Sombra can make it up this mountain." I was worried and embarrassed that I had led the group into this situation.

Irmão spoke calmly. "No worries, brother. We'll make it. We'll carry her if we have to."

Pinga smiled widely and spoke with wry cheer. "Well, we ain't goin' back down!"

We rested, then resumed our climb up the mountain. The dense underbrush thinned, but the terrain grew steeper and more dangerous. Pinga remained cheerful, and Irmão's stoicism never wavered. I tried to stay positive, but my concern deepened when Sombra faltered. She was dehydrated, exhausted, and suffering from the beestings. She stumbled several times. Finally she collapsed and was unable to rise again. The poor dog had so much heart, but she could not go on. Irmão and I lifted Sombra to a flat and shady spot. I sat down beside her and put her head in my lap. Her eyes were half shut and her breath quick and shallow. My heart broke to see her like this, and I knew it was my decisions that had brought us here. I tried to give her the last of my water, but she swallowed only a little.

After a while, we saw that Sombra was not going to rebound anytime soon. We decided I would stay there with her while the other two would continue until they found the car. They would drive the car to the closest point possible and return to us with a rope and water.

So there my dog and I were, perched on the mountainside. Once the guys left, I lifted my gaze and couldn't help but appreciate the beauty and grandeur of the landscape. The great expanse of the Royal Gorge stretched out to the left, with massive Snow Mountain towering downstream and across from us. To the right, the canyon narrowed and branched out with the river's tributary streams. Below us, sheer mountainside plummeted. All around, lush forest contrasted with smooth granite, craggy peaks, and blue sky.

I saw a large bear scat and was surprised that bears wandered such steep terrain. Holding Sombra close, I kept watch. After an hour or so, Pinga and Irmão returned as planned. Sombra had barely recovered and needed a lot of help up the mountain. We tied a rope around her midsection and heaved the ninety-pound dog uphill. Finally, exhausted, we reached the top of the ridge. Grateful and relieved, we lifted Sombra into the Jeep and drove off the mountain.

Despite all of us being safe and more or less sound, I wrestled with guilt and anxiety as we drove home to Sacramento. It was my decisions that had put Sombra and my friends in danger. I felt ashamed of my recklessness, lack of foresight, and selfishness. When I had adventured in the Royal Gorge almost two decades before, it had also been reckless. Being dropped off in the wilderness alone, not bringing food, taking mushrooms, and bushwhacking my way back to civilization had been a dangerous adventure. Nothing bad had happened, and I didn't regret it. I had learned a lot. But back then, nobody depended on me.

Now, things were different. Not only had I led this expedition, but I was a teacher, provider, and leader now. People, and my dog, depended on me. The academy was a significant part of people's lives, and I was key to holding it together. Endangering myself and others was not good leadership. By being reckless, I had neglected my responsibility to the community.

This was a jolting wake-up call, but it also inspired me to remember that what I was doing was bigger than me. I was doing this for the community and to fulfill my lifelong quest to make a difference and do something extraordinary.

My thoughts turned to Carlos Aceituno, our friend from the 2002 State Fair. He had passed away about a year ago, and the news of his death had shaken me deeply. We had not been close friends, but I related to him so much. Like me, he was a non-Brazilian who had trained hard to become an expert in capoeira and related arts. We had both built careers in teaching these arts, passing through similar struggles along the way. I believed that like me, he did this work not only because he enjoyed it but also to improve the world. In our performances together, he had guided his group and mentored mine with patience and humility. Carlos had that fire. He must have had it in order to achieve what he did.

Carlos was gone, and I was still alive. Nobody could help me except myself. Somehow I had to find a way, dig deep, claw out of the hole, bootstrap up. I needed to regain that fire I had in my first years teaching, the fire to push and keep pushing no matter what.

Newly motivated, I went on a guerrilla-marketing spree like in the early days, hitting the streets with stacks of flyers, sending out press releases, adding our name to listings, and organizing performances. Every week I had a long "to do" list of tasks to promote the business, and I crossed items off at a steady pace. Little by little, our enrollment grew.

This all helped revitalized my morale, but I knew there was a bigger, long-term problem. I could not go on being so broke and stressed out all the time. I had to hustle, bust my back, and put in the effort—but I needed to be smarter about it. I needed to apply my energy intelligently, for bountiful return. No more wasting time on things that produced few results. No more working for free or chasing people around for pennies. As my own boss, I needed to figure out a better way, but I didn't have the skills or guidance to lead me to it.

The problem of inconsistent tuition payments remained as a core weakness in my business. I happened to be talking to my friend Mestre Efraim about it, and he urged me to use a professional service for tuition collection. I finally made the leap, and signed up with Member Solutions, a full-service billing company. This made a huge difference in my life, as my income immediately increased and steadied. That winter, for the first time ever, the students paid tuition even if their attendance dropped. I paid all my bills and still had a little left over.

I started saving money and made a plan to invest in real estate someday. This was 2006 and 2007, during the U.S. real estate bubble, and property prices were sky high. I was priced out of the market in California, but kept hoping anyway.

*Me on head facing Mestre Calango, behind us from left, Mestre Rã, Mestre Amen, Mestre Boa Gente, Mestra Suelly, and Mestre Acordeon, Sacramento, 2007.*

I searched for ways to expand my career and develop myself as a teacher. The generous owners of Kovar's Martial Arts, a successful chain of local schools, allowed me to attend their professional training seminar. There I learned about marketing and retention strategies. I enquired at Sacramento State University, and Dr. Goodrich helped me get a job teaching capoeira as a for-credit class. I also started postgraduate studies there for a Master of Science in Physical Education. This reminded me of a line from a capoeira song: *Sou discipulo que aprende, e mestre que da lição*: "I am a disciple that learns, and a master that gives lessons."

My renewed marketing efforts, improved business methods, and an influx of university students grew our group to more than seventy students. Many of my first students were still there, including Caxias, Irmão, Tornado, Bode, Ursinho, Borbulias, and Castanho. We also had a newer generation of talented and dedicated young men and women, including Força, Caçador, Lagartixa, Leopoldão, and Bebida. Together we raised our capoeira and our community to a new level. We organized fundraising parties with live bands, fire shows, and DJs. Our performance troupe had grown in size and skill, and we continued to do shows around the region. A typical thirty-minute Água de Beber set included maculelê, samba de roda, batucada, and capoeira in various forms as well as bits of theater, history, and audience participation.

In 2007 we held our biggest and most successful batizado to date. Through fundraising and registration from around the country, we flew in mestres and friends from as far away as Brazil. It was an honor and a thrill to host legendary teachers including Mestre Acordeon, Mestre Rã, Mestra Suelly, Mestre Amen, and Mestre Boa Gente. Sacramento was officially on the capoeira map.

Despite improvements in my business, finances, relationships, and mood, our academy and my home were still on Del Paso Boulevard, as shady as ever. That had to change. The end of my five-year lease was finally approaching, so I positioned to make some moves.

CHAPTER SEVENTEEN

# Made It

The year 2009 was a busy and pivotal one for me. It included earning my master's degree, finding and securing a new commercial space, closing the Del Paso academy and moving into the new location, buying a house, renovating it, and moving my residence there.

My last semester of post-graduate classes included conducting my thesis study. I studied how different types of verbal feedback affect beginners' learning curves. The skill the subjects learned was the meia lua de compasso kick, with the goal of striking a stationary target. My results supported a newly emerging theory in the motor learning field that suggested students learn better when directed to pay attention to external stimulus, such as a target or apparatus, rather than their own bodies.

After finishing school, I went into full real estate mode, seeking a rental space for the academy and a home to buy. In the last two years, U.S. real estate prices had dropped drastically, especially in places like California. I knew nothing about economics and market cycles. All I knew was that suddenly there were homes I could afford. Some people cautioned that home values might descend further, so it was a bad time to buy. But the numbers and proportions indicated this was a historical opportunity. The only thing I knew about investing was "buy low, sell high." While values might go a little lower, they were already extremely low, so I signed on with an agent and started looking at little fixer uppers around Sacramento.

I also combed Sacramento's streets and avenues looking for empty shops. I had a long list of requirements and my budget was extremely tight, so options were few. The new academy had to be a certain size, centrally located, and in a better neighborhood. It needed to be in a newer building, have easy access to the freeway, and have good parking.

I discovered a large, open shop on Broadway, a couple of miles from our original studio. It was nearly perfect, in a light-industrial building facing a park. The only problem was its size: 3,300 square feet. All that space was great, but the rent would be too high.

My friend Mestre Calango was visiting me. I had first met this Brazilian capoeirista in the early 1990s. He had been a sort of *ronin*, a Japanese term for a martial artist without a master, until Mestre Acordeon had adopted him into the United Capoeira Association. We had become close and maintained a friendship ever since. He was, and still is, an athlete of amazing abilities. Capable of seemingly impossible contortions and flips, his game parallels his personality: joyful and energetic.

Calango occasionally stayed with me in Sacramento for a few days. He was usually looking for work, and I would organize some workshops for him to teach. We'd make berimbaus and caxixis in my yard and go to the river. One day while we were doing errands, I told him about my property search. "At this point, there's only one property I'd show you. It's pretty cool, but I don't think it'll work because it's too big."

*Sacramento News & Review.*

"Bro, let's look at it." Calango spoke with a thick accent. "I tell you what I think."

I drove to Broadway and parked in the parking lot. The building was a tall one-story with large windows facing the street. Calango looked around. "Where, Galego? Where is the space?"

"Right here." I pointed.

Calango gazed at the storefront in amazement. "This is the space you were talking about? Bro, this is awesome! You didn't tell me it was so awesome."

We looked in the windows. Inside was open space with high ceilings. There were no pillars or extra walls, just open space with bathrooms in the back. It was an empty canvas.

Calango peered inside with admiration, then noticed the park across the street and the freeway beyond. "Man, this place is perfect."

I sighed. "I know, but it's big, and that means it will be expensive. I don't know if I can handle it."

Calango looked at me closely. "Galego, this spot is freakin' awesome. This is the spot for you, bro. I'm telling you, get this spot, man. Have faith. You'll make it happen. I believe in you!"

He was right: this property was nearly perfect. A bit bigger than I was hoping for, but better to aim high than low. This was an upgrade, and could be grown into. Plus, realistically I wasn't likely to find anything better. I had been hesitating in doubt, but this was an opportunity I should jump on. I thanked Calango for his encouragement.

I called the property's agent and began negotiating for a lease. Fortunately, the commercial real estate market had crashed along with the residential market. Also, I had excellent credit. I started to explain my business and how it contributed to the community but sensed right away that the owners had no interest. They just wanted someone to pay the rent and not cause trouble. I knew a thing or two about business negotiations by now. Be patient. Know your limit and don't go past it. If you have the chance to make a starting offer, make it lower than your limit so you have room to move, but not so low as to be ridiculous. Don't be emotional or take things personally. Don't appear to need or strongly desire what you're negotiating for. Be prepared to walk away.

My business was small but reliable, with a track record to prove it, and the market was in my favor. I made a lowball offer. The owners showed no willingness to budge from their original, inflated asking rate, so I raised my offer a little. We went back and forth through the agent with offers and counteroffers. At one point I walked away. After a couple of weeks, though, seeing that the space was still vacant, I called the agent again and resumed discussions.

After almost a month, we struck a deal—and it was an excellent deal for me. I would rent at 86 cents per square foot for the first year: $2,850 a month. It was a lot of money for me but a low rate for commercial space in the central district. The rent would increase moderately each year over the course of a five-year lease, which was normal and reasonable. Perhaps my most important victory was four months of free occupancy. For the first of these months, I would still be on Del Paso and building out the new space. For the other three months, I would have income and pay no rent. This was essential to paying for the move.

A month before leaving Del Paso, I received the Broadway keys and did the paperwork for a new business permit, name, taxes, and so forth. Involving other teachers and groups would be key in supporting this bigger space, so in the spirit of inclusiveness and generality, I christened our new academy "Move!"

I made a few offers on homes, and they were declined. Investors, also recognizing opportunity, were paying cash and scooping up all the deals. Finally I found a two-bedroom, two-bath, one-hundred-year-old fixer-upper in a reasonable neighborhood. My agent caught the property just as it came on the market, and I immediately made the highest offer I could: $110,000. After a flurry of communications and paperwork, I became a homeowner.

At the time I barely understood how buying property was one of the only ways someone like me, who didn't make much money, could achieve any kind of wealth and financial security. I'm not saying the American dream of buying a home is always a good idea. As I learned years later, when I sold the same property for almost three times what I bought it for, it depends on timing and the market cycle. I stumbled through the process half by luck but in the end made the kind of money I would never make teaching capoeira. However, it was teaching capoeira that covered that down payment and mortgage that eventually led to security and freedom. A friend called it "the house that capoeira built."

*Halloween Ball, Sacramento, 2010.*

October was a mad dash to transfer everything from Del Paso to my new house or the new academy. My students, friends, and I crated carload after carload to one location or another. Finally, on the last day of the month, I gave up the keys. It had been a long five years at that location. There had been some good times there—classes, batizados, parties, concerts, and more. But overall it had been a trial, and there had been too many hard times. I wouldn't miss it.

So that was it—to my own surprise, everything had worked out. The year ended and things were looking good. But I wasn't out of the woods yet. The same recession that had brought down real estate prices was now catching up to my business—just when all my expenses were rising. And then, due to slashed education budgets, my class at Sacramento State University was cut. I felt a familiar sense of panic and scrambled for ways to make money.

One day during this downturn, my mom called to chat. At first I didn't mention how stressed out I was at the moment, but told her about all the positive developments that had happened.

"I'm so proud of you, Patrick. You made your dreams come true," she said. "And, you get to do what you love."

This was not the first time I had heard this from her, but it still felt good. "You know, I credit you for encouraging me to chase my dreams, Mom. Do you remember how you used to tell me to follow my bliss?"

"Yes, I do. That helped you?"

"Yes. I always wanted to do something unique with my life. When I found capoeira, I knew that was it, and I wasn't afraid to pursue it. And when I moved to Sacramento to start my teaching career, I had to make a leap of faith. My inspiration came from your encouragement to follow my bliss. Now my vision of teaching capoeira is a reality. Thank you!"

"I'm so glad that helped you, and that you've found your bliss!"

We spoke about other things for a while. Eventually she asked, "How is business going?"

"Actually, it is down recently," I admitted. "It's been stressing me out. Sometimes I worry. It wouldn't take much for my business to go under. It's not far from it right now. That'd pretty much mean my whole life falling apart."

"Patrick, I don't think that will happen. You've been doing this for ten years, and you always find a way to make it work. I think as long as you're there to keep it together and still want to keep it going, the business will always survive hard times."

She was right. Ten years is a long time for a small business. Most don't survive that long. No matter what had happened, I had always kept it alive. There would be lean times, but barring catastrophe, the doors would stay open unless I chose otherwise. I just had to tighten my belt and wait out the recession.

*From left, Fabio (partial), me, Rony, Marreta, Pincel, Tigresa, Budinha, Amunka, Cocada, Lucas, Salé, Suelly, Fogueira, Acordeon, Recruta, Mago, Cravo (partial), Sapo, Maluco, Lazarus, Bateria (partial), Lobão, Calango, Sacramento, 2011.*

Eventually the economy recovered and businesses rebounded. My classes grew little by little, and soon Capoeira Água de Beber had more than one hundred students. Because of this, plus bringing in a variety of other classes and arts programs, Move! Studio had become a profitable business and a vibrant cultural hub.

The capoeira group I founded back in 2000 had come a long ways since then. Early on it had been a small band of raggle-taggle young adults. We were from diverse backgrounds but shared a passion for the art, and were fanatical about training and playing capoeira as much as possible. Nowadays, our group is bigger, but less cohesive in a way. People have full lives, and their involvement in capoeira is limited.

*Our third and current academy, Sacramento, 2012.*

Perhaps the period around the late 1990s and early 2000s was a heyday for capoeira in the U.S., or at least for the United Capoeira Association. It was a time of raw enthusiasm, fierce training, and explosive growth. Mestre Acordeon, Mestre Rã, and Mestra Suelly were all at new heights in their careers, and a wave of youthful teachers like myself pressed ahead. We did every demo we could, road-tripped to each others events, and pushed ourselves to get better. Capoeira was our lives.

Some longed for those heady old days, but I felt the new way was better. Maybe there wasn't the same giddy excitement, but it was more healthy and sustainable now. Our group in Sacramento was bigger than ever, and more diverse in age with a bigger kids' program.

*Mestre Acordeon and I, Denver, 2013.*

The U.C.A. was at least as big and as widespread as ever too. Galo and I still had our schools, as did Dondi's student Besouro in Tucson, Guatambu in Los Angeles, India in Miami, Recruta in Hayward, and several others. Mestre Rã had moved back to Brazil, but Mestre Acordeon and Suelly were still running their school in Berkeley. Even as this is written, Mestre Acordeon is reaching new heights. Now he is riding his bicycle from California to Brazil, taking another journey for the ages just shy of his seventieth birthday.

My lifestyle, on the other hand, had changed toward the slow and steady. A distant cry from the far-ranging travels and hardscrabble scarcity of my youth, I had finally become comfortable and secure. Work was steady and rewarding. I owned my house. And I was in my forties now, calmer, and appreciative of a bit of ease. I might have still found myself sleeping under an open sky now and again, but it was largely a soft bed that suited me now.

*My teacher and I, locking horns once again.*

In 2011 we held yet another big batizado, welcoming more than two dozen visiting teachers and hundreds of participants from all over the country. Mestre Acordeon and Mestra Suelly were there as usual, and even Mestre Rã visiting from Brazil. Mestre Amunka participated, sadly on his last trip to Sacramento, as shortly after he passed away. Another blow came a few years later when Dondi, who had recently retired, suddenly passed away as well. The loss of these two towers was a shock to many, and they will be mourned for years to come.

*At Mestre Nenel's academy, Bahia, 2013.*

Our capoeira group was relatively big, and harmonious. We had a beautiful academy, and the business was successful. Best of all, it was sustainable. I was making decent money for the first time in my life, and was doing what I loved. If my career was not unique, at least it was unusual. And, I know my work has made a positive difference in people's lives, and in some small way at least, made the world a better place. For me, this was it—the achievement of my goals, my dream come true. I had made it.

My journey with the art of capoeira has brought me inspiration, purpose, and fulfillment, and I hope this book shares these gifts with its readers. I've learned a lot about the art and culture of capoeira, as well as about how to teach and lead. Most importantly, though, I've learned to be a better human being.

I've learned to be humble. I have an idea now of how little I really know about anything. I have regrets, and I've made mistakes. But I strive not to repeat them. I'm better now at cherishing and caring for people, and I remember not to take our time together for granted. I've learned to recognize and appreciate the good times, endure the bad, and keep both in perspective.

*Capoeira Senzala fiftieth anniversary celebration, Rio, 2013.*

To me, capoeira's greatest gift has been the community it has allowed me to be a part of. It is a rare thing to have people of all walks of life come together willingly and in the spirit of goodwill. And then, for us to participate together in this art that is so potent and unique, allows us to share a special experience. I remember this every time we hold a batizado, when I see newcomers' eyes light up as they see capoeira for the first time.

Capoeira has given me a network of friends around the globe that is invaluable. And our U.C.A is truly a family. Together we've experienced joy, wonder, sorrow, our beloved art, and above all, great camaraderie. And even if on occasion we haven't all seen eye to eye, I still love my capoeira brothers and sisters so much and forever.

Sometimes I've experienced skepticism, but I always knew I would. As a white North American teaching an African Brazilian art, people question my qualifications, motives, and credibility. And rightfully so. But my intent has always been to respect the art, and maintain its integrity. My education was thorough, I only teach what my mestres taught me, and I promote the art for the good of many and not just myself.

My goal is to give more than I receive. I believe I accomplish this by making a positive impact on individuals, building community, and giving back, especially to those who gave us capoeira. Some of the ways my school and I do this is through monetary donations, specifically to the wonderful Projeto Kirimurê, a non-profit set up by Mestre Acordeon to help disadvantaged kids in Bahia, Brazil. We also provide work for capoeira teachers, and sponsor local youths in our classes.

No matter what has happened, I believe it is the same thing that keeps people like me coming back to capoeira. It is that moment when the circle forms, the berimbau calls out, and the game begins. It is that butterfly that still beats its wings in my stomach even after all these years. It's that special alchemy that only capoeira has. It commands my instant and full attention, and rewards me with the never ending possibility of something new.

*Sacramento Carnaval, 2013 (credit fbetophotography.com).*

Mestre Acordeon wrote in his book: "To live the capoeira philosophy requires sweat, mental discipline, sometimes pain, and always the magical experience of kneeling under the berimbau." I believe I've lived this philosophy because to this day when I enter the roda, I still feel that tingling in my spine and the thrill of discovering the unknown that every jogo has the potential for. On a weekly basis, capoeira reminds me of what it means to be alive. It is my passion, my career, and my community. It has helped me make my dreams come true, and kept me young. Thanks to capoeira, I remain, playing in the light.

# Epilogue

I n early 2013, Mestre Acordeon and Mestra Suelly visited us in Sacramento, as they occasionally did for batizados or to teach workshops at our academy. These were occasions for us to catch up and discuss current events. Mestre Acordeon had mentioned on the phone that there was something in particular he wanted to talk to me about. This was normal, and I didn't think much of it.

They drove up to the academy a couple hours before class, and I went outside to greet two friends and mentors of now twenty-three years. "Mestre! Suelly! How are you?" I hugged each of them.

Mestre Acordeon's deep, rumbling voice had lost no richness with age. He was in his late sixties now, but as creative and driven as ever. "I am good, Galego. How are you, old friend?"

"I'm good, Mestre." We entered the academy. I always felt a special pride when my teachers came into this beautiful space.

I had hung a picture of all of us together on a wall. "Aww," said Suelly, "what a nice photo!" Then she noticed a large photo album on my desk.

"Yeah it is," I said. "That album is to commemorate my twenty years in capoeira. You should check it out."

"I'd like to see it," she said.

"Galego," said Mestre Acordeon. "We'd like to talk to you. Can we go somewhere for a coffee?"

"There's a nice café down the street," I said. "We can bring the album."

At the café, we caught up on each other's lives, work, students, and travels. Suelly opened the photo album. There we were at Baker's Martial Arts in the early 1990s, at the old Capoeira Arts Café, in Brazil, and in Sacramento. Pictured were batizados, rodas, performances, and many longtime students and friends. Calango, Amunka, Dondi, Fogueira, Galo, Caxias, Irmão, Bode, Borbulias, Mestre Rã, and many more appeared in the album's photos.

"You've had a good career in capoeira so far, Galego," said Mestre Acordeon. "You've gained a lot of experience and built a strong school here in Sacramento. I'm proud of you."

"Thank you, Mestre."

"Like I said, I want to talk to you about something. As you know, we are planning a big event for this fall in Berkeley, where we will graduate several of our Berkeley students and two of yours."

These students of mine, Caxias and Irmão, would be my first graduated students. Mestre Acordeon and I had already talked about this. "Yes, Mestre. I'm looking forward to it."

"Yes, good, we are looking forward to it also," said Mestre Acordeon. "But Galego, aside from your students graduating, you will have another special role." He paused, looking at me intently. I looked back at him blankly, and then at Mestra Suelly, who had a strange smile on her face.

Now I was curious. "Uhh... Okay, Mestre. Whatever you say, I'll be happy to participate. What's going on?"

After another long pause Mestre Acordeon finally spoke again, this time with that powerful conviction that first impressed me so many years before.

"Galego, you are to become a mestre."

*With Mestra Suelly, Mestre Acordeon, and Mestre Rã at my promotion to mestre, Berkeley, 2013.*

# Acknowledgments

My sincerest gratitude goes to Kathy Benson for her early encouragement, Jennifer Holder for her wise guidance, and Claire Crevey for her expert editing. My deepest thank you also to Len Davisson, Anna Dohnke, Erik Fernandez-Garcia, Kathleen Guerra, Sonya Collier, Chris Coey, Thomas Hilligan, Valerie Hope, Mariam Kaviani, Ubirajara Almeida, Suellen Einarsen, Lori Navarrette, Casio Martinho, Siobhan Hayes, Eugene McNally, Brett and Melissa Chaffins, Arthur Soares, Bryan Castle, Ricky Lawson II, Erica Blyther, Zackrick Cannady, Sharon Firestone-Krasnoff, Maurice Shaw, Gregory Flickinger, Brandon Griffin, Michael Gonçalves Davis, Linda Goodrich, and Amen Santo, for their generous assistance.

# Glossary

Afoxé: An African Brazilian music and dance genre derived from the rhythms of the Orixas, African deities. A group that practices this art.

Água de Beber: Literally "water to drink," a phrase used in several Brazilian songs, and a metaphor for knowledge and learning.

Angoleiro: Someone who practices the Angola style of capoeira. See Capoeira Angola.

Apelido: Nickname.

Armada: An upright spinning kick.

Atabaque: A hand drum of African origin, similar to a conga drum.

Aú: A type of cartwheel.

Aú sem mão: cartwheel with no hands. A side aerial.

Axé: A word of Yoruba origin that means life force or positive energy. Also a popular music and dance genre.

Bahia: The Northeast Brazilian state that is the cradle of African Brazilian culture.

Bahiana: A woman from Bahia.

Bahiano: A man from Bahia.

Banda: A takedown movement in which a capoeirista secures an opponent's kicking leg and sweeps the support leg from underneath him or her.

Barraca: Literally "tent," a small shack from which goods are sold on or near a street or beach.

Batizado: Literally "baptism," an initiation rite of passage for beginning capoeira students.

Batucada: A style of samba characterized by a large percussion troupe. See samba.

Batuque: A martial arts game of African Brazilian origin. Two players in a circle attempt to throw each other to the ground with sweeps and blows.

Bedouin: Desert nomads of North Africa and the Middle East.

Bênção: A straight, pushing kick.

Berimbau: The leading musical instrument of capoeira consisting of a single string bow with a gourd attached as a sound box.

Bodhrán: An Irish hand drum.

Cabeçada: A blow delivered with the crown of the head, a head-butt.

Cachaça: Sugar cane liquor.

Caipirinha: A popular mixed drink in Brazil that contains cachaça, lime, sugar, and ice.

Capoeira: A traditional African Brazilian art form that includes martial arts, dance, acrobatics, music, and ritual in a game between two players.

Capoeira Angola: A style of capoeira that is highly ritualistic and is intended to reflect old-time traditions of the art.

Capoeira Regional: A style of capoeira that is less ritualistic and more athletic. Created by Mestre Bimba.

Capoeirista: A practitioner of the art of capoeira, someone who plays capoeira.

Carnaval: An annual festival derived from the tradition of celebration before the abstinence of Lent.

Chapa giratório: A spinning side kick.

Cintura desprezada: A movement involving two people where one throws the other into an acrobatic flip.

Contramestre: The title and level of a capoeira teacher after professor and before mestre.

Cordão: A cord used as a belt. Its color signifies a capoeirista's rank.

Farol: Lighthouse.

Folha Seca: Literally "dry leaf," an acrobatic movement in which a capoeirista leaps off of one foot and does a backward windmill flip.

Formatura: The graduation of students from a capoeira school.

Forró: A popular partner dance and music genre from Northeast Brazil.

Gaeltacht: The area of northwest Ireland where people still speak Gaelic.

Galego: Literally "Galician," or a person from Galicia in Northern Spain. Used in Brazil colloquially for anyone with light hair and complexion.

Galopante: A blow with an open hand.

Ginga: Capoeira's basic side-to-side step.

Hookah: A water pipe for smoking flavored tobacco.

Jogo: Game.

Litoral: Coastal area.

Macaco: Literally "monkey," a kind of back-handspring.

Maculelê: An African Brazilian folkloric dance involving sticks or machetes.

Malandro: Rogue, rascal, con man.

Martelo: Literally "hammer," a side kick in which the top of the foot strikes horizontally.

Meia Lua de Compasso: Literally "half moon of the compass," a circular kick with the hands on the ground.

Mestre: Master. In capoeira, the highest title and level.

Miudinho: A newer style of capoeira that is highly acrobatic and played in a small space.

Orquestra: Orchestra. The combined musical instruments of capoeira.

Pandeiro: A type of tambourine used in capoeira and samba music.

Parafuso: Literally "screw," a jumping spinning kick.

Pé do Berimbau: "The foot of the berimbau," the place where a capoeira game starts.

Pousada: A hostel or budget hotel (spelled posada in Spanish).

Professor: Professor. In capoeira, a graduated student who teaches.

Quilombos: Communities of runaway slaves in colonial Brazil's backcountry.

Rasteira: A takedown in which a foot sweep trips the opponent.

Real: The Brazilian currency.

Roda: Literally "wheel," the circle in which the capoeira game takes place.

Rodoviária: Central bus station.

Rolê: A low spinning movement typically with hands on the ground.

Ronin: A Japanese term for a warrior without a master.

Samba: Brazil's national dance and music, derived from African roots.

Samba de Roda: A traditional Bahian form of samba. In this style, usually two people dance inside a circle made up of musicians and other participants.

Samba Reggae: Samba fused with Caribbean reggae rhythm.

Senzala: Slave quarters in colonial Brazil. Also the name of a prominent capoeira group started in Rio.

Seqüência: Sequence or choreography of movements.

Trio Elétrico: Large trucks outfitted with sound systems and music acts. Central attractions of Carnaval in Bahia.

Troca de Cordões: Changing of cords, the ceremony in which capoeira students graduate from one level to the next.

Vingativa: Literally "vengeance," a takedown in which an opponent is lifted off his or her feet and thrown to the ground.

Volta por Cima: An acrobatic movement arching backward, landing on the hands, and then kicking the legs over in a kind of walkover.

Made in the USA
San Bernardino, CA
15 January 2019